MARKED for
INTERCESSION

Margie Fleurant

Marked for Intercession
by Margie Fleurant

Printed in the United States of America

ISBN 9781498401838

Scripture quotations taken from the New King James Version. Copyright © 1984 by Thomas Nelson Inc.

www.xulonpress.com

Dedication

This book is dedicated to you, the intercessor, who will lay up treasure in heaven and lives not for this world, but for eternity. This book is also dedicated to my Lord Jesus Christ. Jesus, if it weren't for you, I wouldn't be who I am today, or what I will be in the future.

Acknowledgements

*F*irst, I would like to acknowledge my husband John, whose prayers have much power and whose heart has always been to finance the gospel. Because of your dedication, discipline, and support, I have been able to fulfill the call on my life.

I want to thank my children, Jonathan, Danielle, and Jaclyn. Your words and special letters of encouragement did not go unnoticed. And yes, I did write this book for my children with the hopes that some day you will read it and walk in the light of this revelation.

To my true friends and fellow ministers, people with whom I have had extensive conversations with over the years, both personal and in regards to ministry, I thank you for your time and prayers.

Finally, to my faithful intercessors: you know who you are, those who have faithfully stood in the gap for me, my family, and the call of God in my life.

Order of Chapters

Introduction

*I*n March of 1976 I accepted Christ as my Savior. Six months later I assumed the role of student at what I considered to be one of the greatest bible schools in America. While in attendance there, I learned the principles of God through His written word and discovered that I could stand on His promises every day of my life. Knowledge of this Word, mixed with faith, was the beginning of mountains removed in my life.

In retrospect, I suppose I always had a desire to know God intimately as a Father, a brother, and a friend. I can remember as a small child how I would often sit on a tree stump in my parents' backyard, look up into the breathtaking sky and talk to Him, eager to be familiar with the God who created me! I see now how those moments were not just mere childhood episodes, but divine encounters. Anyway, a few months after bible school, my desire for more of God increased immensely. Although I was filled with the Holy Spirit and spoke with other tongues, I found myself feeling unsatisfied in my new relationship with Christ. I thought, "What could this be?" Psalms 63:1–2 became my heart's cry unto the Father. In it the writer states: "Oh God, thou art my God; early will I seek thee; my soul thirsteth for Thee, my flesh longeth for thee in a dry and thirsty land where no water is; to see thy power and thy glory, so as I have seen thee in the sanctuary."

God, by way of the Holy Spirit, started to expand my prayer life and I eventually began to see the world through His eyes. In my prayer closet, I was shown the needs of the people and how God longs to meet their needs. He showed me cities and nations that were in need of revival, and strongholds that were over them. What I saw affected my heart! As I yielded myself to the Holy Spirit, I found myself crying out on behalf of these people, cities, and nations. I was in tears for the lost. At times, the burden of the Lord moved so strongly in me that I had absolutely no words in articulate speech; only groaning in the spirit.

God spoke to me one day and told me that if I would totally yield to Him, He would use me as an instrument to get His will accomplished here on earth, and that Jesus, the intercessor, would move sovereignly through me. He also said that intercessory prayer would be a major key to one of the mightiest revivals the earth will ever see. There is a great need for this kind of praying in the Body of Christ; God said that He is searching for intercessors that will stand in the gap for people, ministries, cities and nations. I willingly said, "Here I am Lord, flow through me." Hence, I gave birth to this book regarding intercessory prayer. In it I will share all that the Word of God and the Holy Spirit have taught me. I do not know all there is to know on this topic, for the Bible tells us that "we know in part, and we prophesy in part". Therefore, I share only the knowledge I possess. As directed by God, I will attempt to make it as simple as possible, because the prayer of intercession is not to be a mystery or some spooky, far-out practice reserved for the elect few.

I hope you will be open to the Lord as you study the contents of each chapter. Ironically, I once thought that there were very few scriptures referencing the prayer of intercession. Needless to say, I was wrong. The revelation I received in both the Old and New Testaments regarding intercession was indeed life-changing. You see, God never asks us to do anything without showing us how to do it. In this book, I will show you how to be an effective intercessor for Him. Take the scriptures you receive from this book, look them up in the Bible, go into prayer, and let the Holy Spirit teach you Himself.

My prayer for you is that you may know Him and become deeply and intimately acquainted with Him, that His heart would become your heart, and that you would see the world through His eyes. I pray that the eyes of your understanding would be enlightened and that you would see more than you are seeing and hear more than you have heard. In Jesus' Name. Amen.

House of Prayer

Chapter 1

Therefore whoever hears these sayings of Mine, and does them, I will liken him to a wise man who built his house on the rock: and the rain descended, the floods came, and the winds blew and beat on that house; and it did not fall, for it was founded on the rock. (Matt. 7:24–25)

Why didn't the house fall? It did not fall because the man was wise enough to build it upon a good foundation. What was the foundation Jesus was speaking of in this scripture? The foundation is the Word of God, and it is built by hearing and doing God's Word. There has never been so much revelation of the Word of God than in the time in which you and I live. We have found out that the Word of God is relevant for this time. It is alive and powerful. (Heb. 4:12) We know that the Word of God is medicine or health to us spiritually, emotionally, and physically. (Prov. 4:20–23) It works and we can stand on it, for it is a good foundation. These are the last days, and we are coming to the unity of the faith. Because of the Word of God, we are no longer children tossed to and fro and carried about by every wind of doctrine. We are coming to a place of maturity in Christ Jesus. (Eph. 4:11–18) Along with that maturity comes responsibility. We see in Galatians 6:10 that we are collectively the household of faith and are built on the foundation of the apostles and prophets, with Jesus Christ being the Head. Even though storms may come against us, we remain steady. This generation will not crumble under pressure! Churches all over the world are building their ministries on the Word of God and are seeing Him add people who should be saved to their members daily. 1 Corinthians 3:16 states that we, individually, are the temple or the very house of the Holy Spirit. We have built our lives on what the Bible says about us, not what our circumstances look like. When sickness or some type of destruction comes against us, we know how to stand and overcome every time. Why don't we fall? We don't fall because we have built our "house" on God's Word.

Now it says in Isaiah 56:7 that "Even them will I bring to my holy mountain, and make them joyful in my house of prayer; their burnt offerings and their sacrifices shall be accepted upon my altar, for mine house shall be called the house of prayer for all people." Yes, we are to build our lives, "our house", on hearing and doing what the Bible says, but let us take our walk with God one step further. God also desires us to be an individual house of prayer. He said, "My house shall be called a house of prayer." You are equipped to have a deeper fellowship with God, who is your Father, not just through the written Word and by attending church services. This deeper knowledge of God can be developed through intimate times spent with Him in prayer. "Again Jesus began to teach beside the lake. And a very great crowd gathered about Him ... And He taught them many things in parables ... With many such parables Jesus spoke the Word to them as they were able to hear and comprehend and understand. He did not tell them anything without a parable; but privately to His disciples ... He explained everything fully." (Mark 4:1–2, 33, 34) (AMP) Another translation says, "and when He was alone with them He expounded all things to His disciples". Jesus was intimate with His disciples when they were alone with Him. He was able to reveal more of Himself in that private time.

Prayer is your lifeline to God. When you call upon Him, He is always home. "Call upon me and I will answer you." (Jer. 33:3) When you call upon Him, there is never a busy signal. All you have to do is pick up the "phone" and He is there waiting for you. Yes, you are His and He is yours. Prayer is a time of intimate communication with the God of the entire universe; He is in love with you and wants to talk to you. He also wants to hear what you have to say to Him, because He is sincerely interested in you. God will never leave you nor forsake you and will not interrupt you. He will not ignore you and promises to pay attention when you call. "Now my eyes will be open and my ears attentive to the prayer offered in this place." (2 Chron. 7:15)

Before the fall in Genesis, God would come to Adam and Eve for fellowship with them. He enjoyed their company. I think we have it better than Adam and Eve did because they would hear the sound of the Lord God walking in the garden toward them. The Father would come to them. Now, in Christ, we can go directly to God, any time, any day. We do not have to wait for God to come to us. The Father is seeking those whose heart is to worship Him, to come to Him in earnest prayer. We do not have to necessarily enter a church building or certain place to find Him. He is within us, and we are the houses of prayer. He just wants us to respond to His love, and we will because we are not afraid of Him. God, you see, is the very essence of love. He will never fail to respond to those He loves.

There is no limit to the height and depth of the knowledge of who God, the Father, the Lord Jesus Christ, and the Holy Spirit are. Your desire and will to seek Him out is the key to obtaining this knowledge. You are the one who opens and closes the door of fellowship with God. 1 Corinthians 14:15 says, "I will pray."

How much of God do you want? I so often hear people say, "I want more of God." My answer to them is: my friend, God wants more of you. He wants more intimate time with you so He can fill you with His life, His glory, His ideas, and His strength. His plans for you and for all humanity are to bless and prosper, not to harm in any way. The more you give yourself to God in prayer, the more of God you will see. This prayer habit is born out of an act of your will, for He is not going to override your plans. God does not force Himself on anyone. The Bible says that he who comes to God must believe that He will reward those that diligently seek Him. He is waiting for you. Draw near to God and He will draw near to you. (James 4:8) He will in no way cast you out. (John 6:37)

When we read about past revivals, we invariably see that the believers were men and women of prayer and that they prayed not just for themselves or their families but were available to the Holy Spirit in intercession for all people and for all nations. A man is no bigger than his prayer life. In order for revival to happen, it must be generated and fueled by the prayers of the righteous. The swift and powerful movement of the Holy Spirit recorded in the book of Acts was not only initiated by prayer, but fed and sustained by prayer. A movement will only last as long as the spirit of prayer that inspired it.

The Greatest Act of Love

Chapter 2

This is my commandment, that you love one another, as I have loved you. Greater love has no man than this, that a man would lay down his life for his friends.

(John 15:12, 13)

When you received Jesus as your Savior you became "a new creature in Christ Jesus, old things passed away, all things became new." (2 Cor. 5:17) The part of you that was changed was your inner man, or your spirit. You see, you are a spirit. You have a soul (mind, will, and intellect) and you live in a body. Your spirit is what gives you life and breath. This is the part of you that is reconnected with God when you are born again. You are one with Him. You have eternal life within you. Everything you have need of from God is already within you. He has given you wisdom, righteousness, and sanctification. You have all things that pertain unto life and godliness; you are one with Him. The question is, how much of this life of God do you want to tap into and walk in? The sower sows the Word. The result of this truth is reaped differently through different people. Some will walk in it 100 fold, some 60 fold, and others just 30 fold. Some will never walk in any of it. Since we have been born again, we are to be conformed into the image of Jesus. We are to be like Jesus. Our purpose is to allow the life of Jesus to live through us. Jesus did many things in His earthly ministry. He healed the sick, cast out demons, fed the hungry, healed the broken-hearted, and taught truths about Himself and His Kingdom. He spoke of and fulfilled every prophecy about Himself that was written in the Old Covenant. His earthly ministry came to a close when at the cross He bowed His head and said, "It is finished." He who knew no sin became sin for us. He took the penalty of sin for us so that we could have eternal life. He was the second Adam. Jesus became our Intercessor. In order to get to the Father God, we must receive Jesus and His finished work at Calvary. He took our place; He became an intercessor for us. We go to the Father through the Son, by His shed blood.

> He (the Father) saw that there was no man, and won-
> dered that there was no intercessor; therefore, His own
> arm (Jesus) brought salvation. (Isa. 59:16)

While we were yet sinners, Christ died for us. Jesus laid down His life for us, not asking for anything in return. He did it because of His great love for us. He came to the earth as an intercessor. He bridged the gap between God and sinful man. Now, Jesus calls us His own. He calls us His chosen. He calls us His friend.

Jesus taught us that we are to "love one another as I have loved you". He said to love in the same way. What was the greatest act of love that Jesus portrayed? He laid down His life as an intercessor; hence the greatest act of love you can do for a person is to be their intercessor in prayer. Simply stated, prayer for another is unselfish. It is to give of yourself in behalf of another person without any other motive but obedience to God's Word and to the law of unconditional love. We are all called to walk in this type of unconditional love. It is a commandment.

On the third day after Jesus' death on the cross, we know He rose from the dead. He is now seated at the right hand of God the Father, and His ministry continues. He is a High Priest forever, after the order of Melchizedek. We are now under a better covenant with God based upon better promises. Instead of imperfect earthly priests offering up animal sacrifices, Jesus, the perfect Lamb of God, sacrificed Himself once and for all.

> But Jesus, on the other hand, because He continues for-
> ever, holds His priesthood permanently. Therefore He is
> able to save forever those who draw near to God through

Him, since He always lives to make intercession for them. (Heb. 7:24, 25) (NASB)

Right now, Jesus the Intercessor is in us, and through the new birth we have learned that we are to allow His life to flow through us. Again, the Intercessor is in us. He needs to be loosed and let go, for we are to "ever live" to make intercession for others. This should be our goal in life.

In Galatians 2:20 it says, "I am crucified with Christ, nevertheless I live; yet not I but Christ liveth in me." The intercessor is in us. The scripture says, "As He is, so are we in this world." (1 John 4:17) All are called to the ministry of intercessory prayer. This ministry is not a part of the five-fold office call as spoken of in Ephesians 4:11, but it is a ministry; it is a call to prayer. The Spirit of Grace and Supplication has been poured into our hearts by the Holy Spirit. We are the houses of prayer.

The Father is searching for men and women that will pick up the mantle of the power of intercessory prayer. All are called to the ministry of intercession, but few choose to walk in the power of this kind of praying. Will you choose today?

Intercession is a lifestyle that is developed through time and practice. Over time, walking as an intercessor will become as natural as breathing. Eventually, it will become a habit; it just takes accurate knowledge of the Word of God and practice. The Holy Spirit will be your teacher and guide as you yield to this call. It is bringing your body under subjection to the Holy Spirit and praying when you may not feel like praying. Intercession is an act of laying down one's life. Simply stated, you are laying down your time, your interests, your own needs and goals, and taking up His. Walking as an intercessor requires a sacrifice of some portion of the "self life", and taking up the higher life in Him. Don't lay up treasures here on this earth, but lay up treasure and rewards in heaven. The treasures of the earth are only temporary, yet what you do for God will last for all eternity. When you give up the toys of the senses, you will reap the riches of the spirit.

Whenever God asks us to do something, He always has a plan that will bring us blessings in return. As you plant intercession, He will cause others to rise up and pray for you. It is the law of sowing and reaping as spoken of in 2 Corinthians 9:6–10. You may not know whom, but someone somewhere in the world is standing in the gap for you.

Ingredients for Successful Intercession

Chapter 3

Love

> *If I speak in the tongue of men and of angels, but do not have love, I have become a noisy gong or a clanging cymbal. If I have the gift of prophecy and know all mysteries and all knowledge; and if I have all faith so as to remove mountains, but do not have love, I am nothing. If I give my possessions to feed the poor and if I surrender my body to be burned but do not have love, it profits me nothing. Love is patient, love is kind and not jealous; love does not brag and is not arrogant, does not act unbecomingly; it does not seek its own, is not easily provoked, does not take into account a wrong suffered, does not rejoice in unrighteousness but rejoices in the truth; bears all things, believes all things, endures all things. Love never fails.* (1 Cor. 13:1–8) (NASB)

> *Keep yourself in the love of God.* (Jude 1:21)

Intercession must always be born out of a heart of love for God and for people. Love must dominate in intercession. It must be the force behind intercession. The greater the love, the greater the anointing will be as you intercede. We are instructed to "let this mind be in you which was also in Christ Jesus". He gave of Himself out of a heart of love. He gave, expecting nothing in return. His reward came from His

19

only source, His Father. Practicing the prayer of intercession is a way to free yourself from the 'self' life. In this type of prayer, the focus is on the needs of others, not on your own needs. Your needs become secondary. Praying for others is the greatest act of love. It is following after unconditional love. It is following after God's law of love, doing His work, and taking care of His business. My friend, you take care of God's business and He will take care of yours. Love never fails. Seek first the Kingdom of God and all the things you need will be added unto you, good measure, pressed down, shaken together, and running over.

A mature intercessor will not be critical of the needs or shortcomings of others. Instead, he will have compassion for that person. God does not hear the prayers of a critical heart, but He will have the heart of God for a person in need. He will not judge or condemn, but will see the ability of God's power as a way to help that person be all they can be. Love will constrain you to pray until that person is saved, healed or whatever their need may be. Love believes the best in others.

Intercession is not an avenue in which you pray for the vengeance or destruction of a person. It is God's place to vindicate; it is your place to love. Your motivation must be love out of a pure heart with no hidden agenda and no hidden motive. I cannot emphasize this point enough. If you question your attitude or motivation for prayer, your heart is in the right position before God. You are judging yourself and asking God to search your heart. This type of humility before Him is opening up the door of your heart to see as God sees that person. You are keeping yourself pure, and since all prayer is fellowship with God, you will come to know and understand who God is as well.

> Keep yourselves in the love of God, looking for the mercy
> of our Lord Jesus Christ. (Jude 1:21)

As you follow after love, be open for the manifestation of the gifts of the Holy Spirit. Love will see a need while in prayer that otherwise may be hidden. The gifts of the Spirit may operate through a man or woman in prayer as the Spirit wills. (1 Cor. 14:1; 12:7–11) Again, love must be the motivation, not the need to appear "spiritual" because these gifts of the spirit happened to operate through you. Don't ever seek the glory of men. We have seen the manifestation of these gifts in our public church meetings or prayer groups, but they can also operate through the intercessor while in the private place of prayer, where no one else sees or hears. These gifts operate when the intercessor is capable of a love walk that is beyond reproach. Love doesn't tell secrets, doesn't judge or criticize. Love covers a multitude of sin. When God allows you to know something about a person by revelation, it means He can trust you. A relationship is built on trust. He sees how you are faithful in your ability to walk in love and that you will keep this secret He revealed between you and your God. Pray through to the end, believing the best of that person. If you tell another person what God has shown you, you will grieve the Holy Spirit. You have allowed corrupt communication to proceed out of your mouth. Therefore, don't expect the Holy Spirit to flow through you with these manifestations until you truly repent before God. When an intercessor cannot be faithful when given a little, he or she cannot be given more. If you prove faithful when given little, God will continue these manifestations and much more. Without love, your prayers become a noisy gong or a clanging cymbal. With love, your prayers are a delight to the Lord and a sweet fragrance before Him. Of all the ingredients for successful intercession, the greatest of these is love.

Vision

Where there is no vision, the people perish. (Prov. 29:18) (KJV)

I will stand my watch And set myself on the rampart, And watch to see what He will say to me, And what I will answer when I am corrected.
Then the Lord answered me and said: "Write the vision And make it plain on tablets, That he may run who reads it. For the vision is yet for an appointed time; But at the end it will speak, and it will not lie. Though it tarries, wait for it; Because it will surely come, It will not tarry. (Hab. 2:1–3)

Vision comes from two sources: first, from the written Word of God. He has countless promises in His Word. All the promises of God are yes and true. His Word is forever settled and does not change. The vision is written in your heart through the Word of God. Now you have a goal to reach. Again, vision comes from God's Word, which is His heart, and He has a vision. Yes, He has a plan. God is the author and finisher of this plan and He writes this vision in your heart through the Word. As you pray, He makes it plain. You, as a co-laborer with Him, can run with this vision in prayer.

For example, it says in Acts 16:31, "You will be saved, you and all your household." Take this promise and begin to visualize your entire family serving God. Stand on this unchanging promise and don't let go of it! Don't look at what you see in the physical realm, but visualize this promise being fulfilled with the eyes of your spirit; your spirit man has eyes. In your spirit you have the faith to take hold of this promise and through intercession pray it through! Faith is of the heart, and this faith is within you! Your circumstances may say one thing, but don't allow your senses to dictate to you. It says in 2 Corinthians 4:18, "While we look not at the things that are seen, but at the things which are not seen. For the things which are seen are temporal, but the things which are not seen are eternal." In other words, everything in the natural is subject to change. Allow the promise of their salvation to be more real than the present circumstances. The Word of God is the mirror. Look into the mirror and allow what you see to be your focus.

The second source of vision is from a prophetic Word from God. Prophecy is foretelling, or forth telling. You may receive a word of wisdom, which is something in the future. (1 Cor. 12:6–10) How is this vision received? It can be received by hearing prophetic preaching or teaching at a church service, or it can come directly to you through a prophetic utterance by a man or woman of God; or it may come as a word of wisdom directly to you as you pray privately. In this context I am not talking about an open vision, although a person who stands in the office of a prophet does indeed have open visions. This type of manifestation is less frequent to the intercessor and may happen once in a lifetime, if at all. Vision can be a prophetic word from God through an individual or in a dream. It can come as a knowing in your spirit. It can manifest as an inner conviction or the consistent voice of your conscience. It could be a scripture that comes to you as a *rhema* from God, as seen in Chapter 6.

> And there was a prophetess, Anna, the daughter of Phanuel, of the tribe of Asher. She was advanced in years, and had lived with her husband seven years after her marriage, and then as a widow to the age of eighty-four. She

never left the temple, serving night and day with fasting *wow*
and prayers. At that very moment she came up and began
giving thanks to God, and continued to speak of Him
to all those who were looking for the redemption of
Jerusalem. (Luke 2:36–38) (NASB)

Now Anna stood in the office of the prophet. (Eph. 4:11) Prophets
are men and women of prayer: All manner of prayer, especially intercessory prayer. (Eph. 6:18) (AMP). Anna fulfilled her ministry both privately and publicly. Her public ministry was prophetically speaking of
Him that was to come. She was speaking of the coming Redeemer; she
was speaking of Jesus. Her private ministry prophetically was one of
prayer. Anna served her God with fasting and prayer. She gave birth to
that prophetic word that she received from God. Part of her call was to
pray for the fulfillment of God's plan. Anna had vision, and she purposed
within herself to pray until she saw it come to pass in her lifetime. My
question is, how long did Anna pray? How long did she carry that vision
in her heart? It might have been years. It might have been months or days.
I don't know, but I do know this: if God has put a vision in your heart,
don't let go of it. May His will be done on earth as it is in heaven. Don't
faint, and don't lose hope (Luke 18:1) God is not a man that He should
lie, nor the son of man that He should repent. Has he spoken? Won't He
make it good? (Num. 23:19)

Desire

Successful intercession requires desire. It must be burning. First, we
must have a burning desire for God, to know Him, and to become deeply
and intimately acquainted with Him. We must have a burning desire for
all to be saved and to come to know the saving knowledge of Jesus Christ.
We must have a burning desire for a move of God in the earth. Now vision
will help to create desire, and if you don't have vision, ask God to give it
to you as He did for Habakkuk in the second chapter. He will answer
you just as He answered Habakkuk. He will work it in you. God said, "I
am all the while at work in you to will and to do of My good pleasure."
As you commit to Him your time, and yield and delight in Him, He will
give you the desires of your heart. His desires will become your desires.

Ask Him to open up the eyes of your understanding so that you can see as He sees. He will answer your prayer; God is neither deaf nor hard of hearing. Ask Him for a heartfelt desire to see His will accomplished in the earth. Over time, your vision will become His vision. What you will be shown from His heart will affect your heart. Prayer not only changes things, but also changes you. You'll find that your desires will change. What used to be important to your selfish nature will become less and less important as you grow in this relationship through prayer. It says in Jeremiah 33:3, "Call upon Me and I will answer you and show you great and mighty (hidden) things, which thou knowest not." When you begin to see these great and mighty things that He desires to do in your family, in your church or in your nation, you will look forward to your prayer time. Your motivation for prayer will come from within. Your desire for God will be stronger than wasting time over some of the foolish things we have spent our time on in this world.

Faith

Now faith is the assurance [the confirmation, the title–deed] of the things we hope for, being the proof of things we do not see and the conviction of their reality [faith perceiving as real fact what is not revealed to the senses]. (Heb. 11:1) (AMP)

Now faith is. Faith is now; therefore there is no time or distance in the spirit realm. As an intercessor you will see things accomplished in the spirit first before you see visible results in the natural, physical realm. As an intercessor, you must walk by faith and not by sight. You must hold fast the confession of your faith without wavering; simply stated, watch what you say with your mouth. Life and death are in the power of the tongue. Don't speak death to answered prayer by the words of your mouth. Faith is released through your words. "With the mouth confession is made unto salvation." God used His words to speak the World into existence; faith is released with your words. An example is Zacharias in Luke 1:11–64. God gave Him the promise. Zacharias questioned what was spoken to him by the angel. Supernaturally he was silenced and unable to speak until the day his son John was born. Once there is breakthrough in intercession and your season of prayer for this particular assignment is complete, speak only the end result; call those things that be not as though they were. (Rom. 4:17–21)

What if you don't sense anything? What if you are unaware of any change at all? Again, that is where strong faith comes in. When God told Abraham that He was going to be the father of many nations, he did not waver. He was about one hundred years old and His wife Sarah's womb was dead. Yet he considered not the circumstances. He considered not problem. He considered not his feelings. He staggered not at the promise of God through unbelief, but was strong in faith and gave glory to God. He was fully persuaded that what God had promised, He was able also to perform. What does God's Word say about prayer? He said in James 5:16, "the effectual prayer of a righteous man avails much." He said, "I will hasten My Word to perform it." (Jer. 1:12) He said, "My eyes will be open and my ears attentive unto the prayer that is made in its place." (2 Chron. 7:14,15) God hears you when you pray, whether you 'see,' sense, feel or hear a scripture that is given to you in your heart in your moment of silence after you have given yourself over to Him in intercession. That is where faith comes in. The intercession or that particular need may not as of yet be finished. Pick the prayer burden up again the next day, but know by faith that your prayers did produce results. Remember, we walk by faith and not by sight. Without faith it is impossible to please God. When you come to God you must believe that He is, and He will reward those that diligently seek Him.

Preparing the Way

Chapter 4

The voice of one crying in the wilderness: "Prepare the way of the Lord; Make straight in the desert, A highway for our God. Every valley shall be exalted and every mountain and hill brought low; The crooked places shall be made straight and the rough places smooth; The glory of the Lord shall be revealed, and all flesh shall see it together; For the mouth of the Lord has spoken." (Isa. 40:3–5)

The voice that is crying in the wilderness is the voice of the intercessor. Through the avenue of prayer, he is the one speaking the Word of God in the dry place that is in need of spiritual water. He is the one speaking on behalf of another. He is the one speaking on behalf of a city or a nation. He is the one preparing the spiritual atmosphere.

We know that this scripture is literally talking about the prophet John the Baptist. For a moment let us look at this scripture in the context of the prayer of intercession. What was the ministry of John the Baptist? What did he do? He was the one who went before Jesus and prepared the way. By the time Jesus (who is the Word of God) came on the scene, people were expectant to see just who this man Jesus was. Their hearts had been prepared to hear what He had to say, and the people gladly received Him. John called the people to repentance and then Jesus came as the Word made flesh. Intercession prepares the way in the same manner, only in the spirit. Intercession goes into the spirit and prepares the hearts of people. This type of prayer puts people in a favorable position to receive the Word of God. 2 Thessalonians 3:1 says, "Pray for us, that the Word of the Lord will have free course." Intercession prepares the way on behalf of an individual who is in need of salvation. Intercession prepares the way prior to a church service or conference. If the way has not been prepared, then the road up ahead will be rough and hard. It will be hard for the Word of God to go forth. It will be more difficult for the people hearing the teaching to receive what is being spoken. The prayer of intercession aids in removing obstacles that may get in the way of success. Where the way has been crooked, intercession will unwind that road so that it is straight and clear. Let's say that this road is a highway. It takes work to build a physical highway. It also takes work in prayer to build a highway for our God. It takes discipline, dedication, labor, and time. My friend, God is looking for co–laborers that will work with Him in building this highway. This highway is for His Word so that it will have free course.

Intercession will build that highway for our God. This is a highway that cannot be built by "might, nor by power," but by the Spirit of the Lord working through us. 2 Corinthians 6:1 says that we are workers together with Him, or laborers with God. We work together. Men and women have to be willing and obedient to this call to prayer. God and man have always worked together. Lets say you are driving down a highway that is crooked and that has many mountains, valleys, and rough places. It goes without saying that you must put forth much more physical effort in order to reach your final destination; you must concentrate on the road. You will have to apply the brakes as you come down the steep mountain and into the valleys. You may have to accelerate up the mountain, which will take a little longer than if the road were flat. This type of driving can become frustrating because over a long period of time it is physically and mentally tiring. You need great concentration. What if this highway were populated with deer? Deer can jump out onto the highway at any time without warning. Serious injury may result to you and your vehicle. This will surely delay you from reaching your final destination. Now if the road has been properly prepared before you, how will your trip be? The workers would have had to use their equipment and special tools to fill the potholes and flatten out the rough areas of the road. With proper equipment the road can be much smoother. The hills and valleys can be properly excavated. You, the driver will experience not only a much smoother ride, but you will reach your destination much quicker. You will also experience less stress from the trip.

If the way has been prepared in the spirit ahead of time through intercession, the Spirit of God will have freedom to manifest. The Word of the Lord will have 'free course'. You will see quicker results and those receiving the Word will be more receptive.

> Those from among you shall build the old waste places; you shall raise up the foundations of many generations; And you shall be called the repairer of the breach, the restorer of streets to dwell in. (Isa. 58:12)

This scripture speaks of the work of intercession. Intercession prepares the way before you. Intercession builds up the old waste places. You become a repairer of the breach, the restorer of the paths to dwell in. You 'bridge the gaps'. You 'fill in the pot holes'. What happens after the way has been prepared? The glory of the Lord will be revealed. The glory of the Lord is the manifested presence of Jesus.

Tilling the Ground

Chapter 5

The sower sows the word. And these are the ones by the wayside where the word is sown. When they hear, Satan comes immediately and takes away the word that was sown in their hearts. These likewise are the ones sown on stony ground who, when they hear the word, immediately receive it with gladness; and they have no root in themselves, and so endure only for a time. Afterward, when tribulation or persecution arises for the word's sake, immediately they stumble. Now these are the ones sown among thorns; they are the ones who hear the word, and the cares of this world, the deceitfulness of riches, and the desires for other things entering in choke the word, and it becomes unfruitful. But these are the ones sown on good ground, those who hear the word, accept it, and bear fruit: some thirtyfold, some sixty, and some a hundred. (Mark 4:14–20)

The eyes of the Lord run to and fro through the whole earth seeking out intercessors. We are the temple of the Holy Spirit, therefore, the house of prayer. Jesus the Intercessor is within us. He wants someone that He can just pray through. He looks for someone who will hook up with Him and allow His spirit to flow freely through. He is looking to pray through us. The Holy Spirit knows exactly what the mind of the Father is. He knows exactly what needs prayer.

Prayer is one of the keys that unlock the door to the manifested glory of God. Prayer is one of the keys that will unlock miracles. Prayer is one of the keys to successful ministry here on earth, not just for the local church but also for the universal church. We possess the land through intercession. We go into the spirit realm and take what was lost in the fall and is now restored in Jesus. We talked about how intercession goes before us and prepares the way for the Word. Prayer opens the door for the Holy Spirit to convict and convince the world of their need for a savior, Jesus of course being the only Savior. As you intercede for someone, they will see Jesus for who He really is. The Bible says that "people perish for a lack of knowledge". (Hosea 4:6) If the world knew the goodness of God, it would lead them to acceptance of Jesus Christ. Intercession influences a hearer to see and know Truth, and their repentant heart is the result. Intercession makes a highway straight for our God.

As you set yourself to answer the call to prayer on the behalf of your city, your nation or other nations, do not be surprised if God imparts vision through a *rhema* word. We have the scriptures that are the foundation of all our prayer requests. This is the written word of God that we can stand on. We take the need to the Word of God, agree with what He says, and present it before the Throne Room. We will go into greater depth on how to pray the scriptures in a later chapter. There are times, though, when a scripture or scriptures "light up" or "jump out" at you when you read your Bible. It is a word in season for you, your present need, or it may be for the specific area for which you are in intercession. It may even be a prayer assignment. He is giving you vision. With that vision, if you will, He will call upon you to pray. I call this a prayer assignment. God takes His written word (*logos*) and illuminates it to you. This particular scripture or scriptures then become a spoken word in this season or this time (*rhema*).

In January of 1981, God called me first to the east coast where I would begin full-time ministry. As I sought Him regarding this area of the nation, He gave me a vision or revelation of what He wanted to accomplish and what my small part would be in the fulfillment of this vision.

> 'Thus says the Lord God: "On the day that I cleanse you
> from all your iniquities, I will also enable you to dwell
> in the cities, and the ruins shall be rebuilt. The desolate
> land shall be tilled instead of lying desolate in the sight

of all who pass by. So they will say, 'This land that was desolate has become like the garden of Eden; and the wasted, desolate, and ruined cities are now fortified and inhabited.' Then the nations which are left all around you shall know that I, the Lord, have rebuilt the ruined places and planted what was desolate. I, the Lord, have spoken it, and I will do it. 'Thus says the Lord God: "I will also let the house of Israel inquire of Me to do this for them: I will increase their men like a flock. Like a flock offered as holy sacrifices, like the flock at Jerusalem on its feast days, so shall the ruined cities be filled with flocks of men. Then they shall know that I am the Lord." (Ezek. 36:33–38)

You can use this scripture for your city or for your nation, for it will apply. Allow me to break these scriptures down. They have a prophetic meaning that relates to us today, not just for that time. He said, 'I will cause you to dwell in the cities, and the wastes shall be built.' Intercession will build our cities, not in a natural, physical manner but in the spirit. What has lain dormant will be built. What was once a waste area will be built again. What has been in ruins will be rebuilt. Then what is done in the spirit will manifest in the natural, physical realm. Through the prayers of the saints the land will be tilled. Intercession tills the ground. It tills the atmosphere of your city, as well as the hearts of men and women. Our opening scripture spoke of different types of ground. The prayer of intercession prepares the soil of the atmosphere, or the soil of the individual hearts of men. When the seed of the Word of God is sown into these areas, the ground will have been prepared because of prayer. The Holy Spirit working through the heart of an intercessor is watering and wooing that individual to Jesus. He waters the seed of the Word of God, and as a result, the ground is softer and more pliable. When you are planting seeds in the soil of the earth, if the ground has not been properly prepared, the seed won't produce a harvest. If some of the seeds germinate and there are roots left in the soil, the weeds will grow again and choke the harvest. Sometimes we want a temporary remedy from the weeds in our gardens, and instead of digging up the roots, we cut off the top of the weed. We are lazy and want a quick fix. It looks good for a while, but eventually they will grow again because we did not take the time to do the work necessary in the beginning to ensure a pure, clean harvest. Look at this analogy in the light of intercession. The work is done in the spirit, in the prayer closet. Yes, it is work. We are co–laborers together with Him in this harvest. We must work with Him and do it God's way. We all don't know everything about the spirit realm and how it works. The Holy Spirit knows all about this unseen realm. It takes the foundation of the Word of God and faith in continuing the work of God in the earth. God is not leading us on a blind path to never–never land. There are rules and laws of the spirit. Through intercession we deal with the soil. Some people don't know they even have any roots. There may be roots of bitterness. What makes a person crumble under the pressure of persecution? What could possibly influence a person to love the power of money more than God? I don't always know what keeps a person hard against the Gospel, but the Holy Spirit certainly does. Yield to Him through prayer and the Holy Spirit, who knows all things, will deal with the roots. When the way has been prepared and the ground tilled, you will see a beautiful harvest. In regards to a city the inhabitants will be a harvest of people that have been born–again and are the new believers that will fill our churches. The churches will be filled with flocks of men and women hungry to hear the truth.

Where Do I Begin?

Chapter 6

Remember this: he who sows sparingly and grudgingly will also reap sparingly and grudgingly, and he who sows generously (that blessings may come to someone) will also reap generously and with blessings. Let each one 'give' as he has made up his own mind and purposed in his heart, not reluctantly or sorrowfully or under compulsion; for God loves (He takes pleasure in, prizes above other things, and is unwilling to abandon or do without) a cheerful (joyous, "prompt to do it") giver, whose heart is in his giving.

(2 Cor. 9:6–7) (AMP)

There are several types of prayer spoken of in the Word of God. (Eph. 6:18 AMP) This book is about just one of those prayers, intercessory prayer. You can make intercession your priority in your prayer time. God will reward those who are faithful intercessors. As you begin walking as an intercessor, purpose in your heart to be a doer of the Word and not a hearer only. (James 1:22) As you draw near to God, He will draw near to you. (James 4:8) Sow purpose in your heart that you are not going to give of yourself grudgingly, nor of necessity, but cheerfully. Sow to the things of the Spirit and you will reap the things of the Spirit. My friend, you are laying up treasure in heaven.

> Do not gather and heap up and store up for yourselves treasures on earth, where moth and rust and worm

consume and destroy, and where thieves break through and steal. But gather and heap up and store for yourselves treasure in heaven where neither moth nor rust nor worm consume and destroy, and where thieves do not break through and steal. For where your treasure is, there will your heart be also. (Matt. 6:19–21) (AMP)

At first you may feel a little apprehensive, but I encourage you to just relax. The Lord will develop you from your starting point. The first thing I suggest is to find a quiet room where you know you have absolute privacy and there are no distractions. Present yourself to God as a house of prayer and in obedience to His Word. (Rom. 12:1) My initial experience was not unlike the above. When I began to walk as an intercessor, I remember how I took the scripture *literally* where it said to "go into the closest and shut the door". You see, I had a walk–in closet that I loved to go into and I would shut the door and turn out the light and pray. I wasn't married nor had any children at the time, so I wouldn't answer the phone. I shut the door on the world, the distractions, and sometimes if I had my favorite food in the refrigerator I had to shut my mind off to that, too! I had purposed in my heart to not open that door until I had finished what I had on my prayer list.

When you first begin to bring your body under subjection to the Holy Spirit, your body and mind will come up with many excuses for being distracted. Train your body and mind to be quiet; yield to your inner man. This is the part of you that is hungry for God, your inner man wants to be trained in godliness. Don't listen to your body or the dictates of your mind. Bring your body under subjection to the Spirit and the Word (1 Cor. 9:27), and after several consistent times of prayer, your mind and your body will quiet down. I just set myself like a flint, and decided I was going to pray! Paul the apostle said, "I will pray". (1 Cor. 14:15) By an act of your will you are entering into the prayer closet. I would not let anything stop me. I was determined to be well pleasing to God. (Rev. 5:8) I wanted to be intimate with God more than anything on this earth. One day as I was praying, I kept saying, "God, I want more of you". He responded back to me and said, "you don't need more of Me; I need more of you". You must realize that everything that God has and is available to us. We just need to press into Him and receive all that He is. When we seek Him, we will find Him. (Luke 11:9, 10) Even if you pray and it seems dry, don't quit. Keep pressing in. You will come to a place where there is what I call a 'breakthrough.'

I made the determination that I would make prayer a priority in my life. (Matt. 6:33) At this stage of development, a closet was the place that helped me in the discipline of prayer. I felt closed in with God. Now I have an office where I do all of my praying and studying, so when the children go to school, I devote myself to the priority of the day as the Holy Spirit leads me. I am able to close myself in, even though I am in a bigger space. I am not as easily distracted as I was when I first began my life as an intercessor. I now also have children, so when the phone rings I make sure I check the number so if my family has any type of need I will be available to them.

The exercise of prayer is similar to the exercise of your physical body. Let's say you wanted to get in shape. Normally, the initial workouts are the toughest because your physical conditioning at this point is probably very poor. Therefore, you do not want to over exert yourself. If you can only do fifteen minutes of aerobics or weights, then you begin there. You will find that as you remain diligent, the length of each workout will increase because your stamina increases. In order to achieve consistent progress you simply must first show up at the gym! There you will get the necessary guidance from a qualified fitness instructor, someone who knows more than you regarding how to get in shape. This person will help you put together an effective exercise program. After several weeks of training, you will begin to notice results. Your physical appearance will begin to transform into the desired outcome. In actuality, the change began in your body after the first workout and you just couldn't see it! The same is true when you begin any prayer program. As you spend time in His presence, you are being transformed.

> And all of us, as with unveiled face, (because we) continue to behold (in the Word of God) as in a mirror the glory of the Lord, are constantly being transfigured into His very own image in ever increasing splendor and from one degree of glory to another, (for this comes) from the Lord (who is) the Spirit. (2 Cor. 3:18) (AMP)

At first you will not notice how you are changing, but over time you will notice a transformation in your love walk. You will notice a transformation in your attitude or your response to life's challenges. You may even notice a greater sensitivity to His voice, or you will carry a tangible awareness of His presence and you will have an overall greater peace in your daily life.

> Be anxious for nothing, but in everything by prayer and supplication, with thanksgiving, let your requests be made known to God; and the peace of God, which surpasses all understanding, will guard your hearts and minds through Christ Jesus. (Phil. 4:6, 7) (NKJV)

While following a consistent program of physical exercise, you will find that your body will eventually begin to 'crave' working out. Diet is also important; eating the right food for your body type will produce positive results. After you have some knowledge of how your body works, you will then be able to develop your own program, one that fits your lifestyle! There are days when you are motivated to work out and then there are days you just do it because you know it is what your body needs in order to be healthy and for you to look your best. We do not allow our body to dictate to us; we tell it what to do. Your body and your mind may make all kinds of excuses as to why you cannot pray today. Just do it! You will find over time that you will begin to 'crave' prayer. Prayer goes from sacrifice to joy, from desire to discipline to delight. Your spiritual diet is also important. Meditate on the Word of God. (Prov. 4:20–23) Know who you are in Christ, and know what the Bible promises. A balanced Christian should maintain a life in prayer, and have consistent devotional time in the Word of God. (2 Tim. 2:15) As you yield yourself to God as a house of prayer, the rewards will extend into all of eternity; your works while here on earth will follow you. (Rev. 14:13)

> For physical training is of some value (useful for a little), but godliness (spiritual training) is useful and of value in everything and in every way, for it holds with it promise for the present life and also for the life which is to come. (1 Tim. 4:8) (AMP)

After I shut the closet door, I would enter into worship. I put my focus on Him who sits on the throne, and unto the Lamb; I would worship Him in the beauty of holiness. I used my spiritual imagination. (Isa. 26:3) I pictured my heavenly Father high and lifted up! (Rev. 19) I imagined myself with all the saints of heaven worshipping Him! (Eph. 2:6) In the Spirit that is exactly what we are doing! We are just in our 'earth suits.' We do not have on our heavenly bodies as of yet. Our citizenship is already in heaven. There is no time or distance in the spirit. Eternity is in our hearts. I knew He was right there with me in the closet. I was not alone because He was there with me. (Heb. 13:5; Matt. 28:20) I do not need to see Him with my physical eyes to know that He is there with me in the spirit. (John 20:29) Worship is important to the intercessor. Worship is refreshing and builds you up; it renews your strength. (Isa. 40:28–31)

It is important to the intercessor to be balanced in his or her prayer life. Your prayer time cannot all be intercessory prayer. The prayer of worship fills you up, while intercession is giving out. It is important to keep a watch on your own personal energy level. Maintain a balance of intercession and worship.

After the prayer of worship, allow the Holy Spirit to search your heart and reveal to you if there is any sin you have not confessed in your life. If there is, confess your sin and ask for forgiveness. (Ps. 51:10; 1 John 1:9) Afterwards, I would always pray first for all those in authority, because that is what the Bible says. (1 Tim. 2:1–4) I then had a prayer list of people and needs. I would pray according to the scriptures that met those specific needs. I set my goal to pray for one hour. (Matt. 26:40) At that time, I would try to pray daily for one hour. If I was unable to pray for a day or for the allotted time I had set for myself, I did not fall into condemnation or guilt. Prayer should be born out of love, not of necessity; therefore if I didn't pray, I did not feel that I was no longer in right standing with God. That is a lie! Yes, God loves us unconditionally and delights in us as we delight in Him, but never go into His presence grudgingly or out of guilt, because the devil would love to torment you with thoughts of guilt and condemnation if you have missed your prayer time. Go in with faith and expectation. God loves a cheerful giver.

After developing for about a year in the discipline of prayer, God spoke to me one day and said, "The way you are led by My spirit in the everyday affairs of life, so I want to lead, guide and direct you in your prayer closet. Don't always come into My presence with your prayer list. Allow Me to develop you in prayer with the help of the Holy Spirit."

> For all who are being led by the Spirit of God, these are sons of God. (Rom. 8:14) (NASB)

This opened up a whole new place for me in my walk with Him in the secret place. This is when the gifts of the Spirit began to operate in my times of prayer. I learned to follow the anointing in prayer and pray for the needs He put on my heart instead of what I always saw before me in the natural realm. (John 16:13) This is when I would be directed to pray for certain nations or cities. I would be directed to pray for people that I may have known personally, but had no natural knowledge of their need. The Holy Spirit knows all things and He needed someone to pray through as the assignments would present themselves. Our priorities are not always God's priorities. Twenty years later, I learned that this type of intercession had been given a name among the church world as 'prophetic praying'. I would spend time worshiping Him first, find out what He said needed prayer, and pray accordingly. That is not to say I did not go into intercession with specific needs that I saw before me. We must follow after the Holy Spirit. If He has no specific direction, there are things we just know need prayer. We then release those requests before the throne room of grace and expect results.

> Let us therefore come boldly to the throne of grace, that we may obtain mercy and find grace to help in time of need. (Heb. 4:16) (NKJV)

Exercising Kingdom Authority

Chapter 7

But even if our gospel is veiled, it is veiled to those who are perishing, whose minds the god of this age has blinded, who do not believe, lest the light of the gospel of the glory of Christ, who is the image of God, should shine on them.

(2 Cor. 4:3, 4)

*I*n the beginning, man had dominion over the earth. He was to tend and keep guard over the garden; he had complete dominion and authority given to him by God. Adam was the ruler. God's only request was that he not eat from the tree of the knowledge of good and evil. This was God's command of complete obedience. (Gen. 2:15–17) God also knew he had an enemy, his name being Satan (he used to be called Lucifer). Lucifer chose to rebel against God and his name was changed to Satan. Lucifer led the worship in heaven; he was lifted up in pride and instead of God receiving the glory, he wanted to be worshipped. (Ezek. 28:11–19) At Lucifer's rebellion, two–thirds of the angels fell with him. They became the evil spirits, devils, principalities, powers and rulers of the darkness of this world that we read about in Ephesians 6:12.

God knew that Satan was roaming about and wanted to rule Eden, the garden of God. God not only wanted Adam to obey Him, He also wanted to protect Adam. It was Adam's responsibility to keep Satan out. Through Adam's disobedience to God, Satan gained entrance into the earth. Adam opened the door and let him in. He lost his God-given dominion and authority. Satan then became the ruler, the king, and the god of this world. In Luke 4:6, we see Jesus being tempted by the devil in the wilderness. "And the devil said to Him, 'I will give you all this domain and its glory, for it has been handed over to me and I give it to whomever I wish.'" This was a true statement or this temptation would not have been real. Satan is here legally. Adam gave him legal entrance into this world. Jesus came into this world as the 'second Adam'. (1 Cor. 15: 45–47) Jesus not only came to restore us back into right standing with His Father, He also came to take back the dominion and authority that was lost in Adam. Jesus has now given that authority to the believer through His death, burial, and resurrection.

> Therefore, since the children share in flesh and blood, He Himself likewise also partook in the same, that through death He might render powerless him who had the power of death, that is, the devil, and might free those who through fear of death were subject to slavery all their lives. (Heb. 2:14–15)

> The Son of God appeared for this purpose, to destroy the works of the devil. (1 John 3:8)

> Having spoiled principalities and powers, He made a show of them openly, triumphing over them in it. (Col. 2:15)

> I am the first and the last; I am He that liveth and was dead, and behold, I am alive forevermore. Amen. And I have the keys of hell and of death. (Rev. 1:17, 18)

> All power is given unto me in heaven and on earth. Go ye therefore and make disciples of all nations, baptizing them in the name of the Father and of the Son and of the Holy Ghost, teaching them to observe all things whatsoever I have commanded you; and lo, I am with you always, even unto the end of the world. (Matt. 28:18–20)

The Word of God is clear and speaks of itself. Through His death and resurrection, Jesus gave the dominion and authority back to the church. We now have authority over the devil. The authority is not in us, but in the name of Jesus. We use the name of Jesus and Jesus is there to back up His name with results. John 14:12, 13 in the Amplified translation says, "I assure you, most solemnly tell you, if anyone steadfastly believes in Me, he will himself be able to do the things that I do; and he will do even greater things than these, because I go to the Father. And I will do, I myself will grant, whatever you may ask in My name (presenting all I Am), so that the Father may be glorified and extolled in (through) the Son." Through the name of Jesus the authority is released. The reason I am giving you so much scripture in this chapter is because you must have faith in the name of Jesus when you pray. "His name through faith in his name...has given this man perfect soundness in the presence of you all." (Acts 3:16) Jesus said in Mark 16:17, "And these signs shall follow them that believe, in My name they shall cast out devils."

Through the name of Jesus, authority over the powers of darkness is exercised. The devil is brought down whether it is on behalf of an individual, a church, a family, a city or a nation. This authority is for all believers to exercise. The believer possesses the keys, which is the symbol of authority on this earth. This authority is not just for a minister to exercise when he prays for his congregation, in a prayer line, or at a hospital visit when one is sick. You, the intercessor, can exercise this authority when you are physically absent from the person or place in which is the target of your faith in prayer. You don't have to physically touch them. You don't have to live in the city or the nation for which you are in intercession. There is no time or distance in the spirit. Paul said, "Though I be absent in the flesh, yet I am present in the spirit." (Col. 2:5)

> Therefore God also has highly exalted Him and given Him the name which is above every name, that at the name of Jesus every knee should bow, of those in heaven, and of those on earth, and of those under the earth, and that every tongue should confess that Jesus Christ is Lord, to the glory of God the Father. (Phil. 2:9–11)

Notice this scripture says every knee must bow and every tongue must confess that Jesus Christ is Lord. Every knee will bow to the Lordship of Jesus: everyone in heaven, on earth, and under the earth. In context with this chapter, every devil must respond to the name of Jesus that is spoken from the mouth of the believer's prayer on behalf of another. We represent Jesus in the earth. We have the keys! We have the power of authority given to us by God. When exercised, this authority will produce results in behalf of humanity. Never underestimate the power of the name of Jesus. Jesus defeated the devil, and every time you speak His name, he is afraid and must bow. The powers of darkness have no choice; it is finished. We simply take our place as His representatives. As an intercessor, you represent Him on behalf of another. The enemy must release the object of your prayer.

Lord, Teach us to Pray

Chapter 8

Now it came to pass, as He was praying in a certain place, when He ceased, that one of His disciples said to Him, "Lord, teach us to pray, as John also taught his disciples." So He said to them, when you pray, say: Our Father in heaven, Hallowed be Your name. Your kingdom come. Your will be done on earth as it is in heaven. Give us day by day our daily bread. And forgive us our sins, for we also forgive everyone who is indebted to us. And do not lead us into temptation, but deliver us from the evil one." And He said to them, "Which of you shall have a friend, and go to him at midnight and say to him, 'Friend, lend me three loaves; for a friend of mine has come to me on his journey, and I have nothing to set before him'; and he will answer from within and say, 'Do not trouble me; the door is now shut, and my children are with me in bed; I cannot rise and give to you'? I say to you, though he will not rise and give to him because he is his friend, yet because of his persistence he will rise and give him as many as he needs. (Luke 11:1–8)

The disciples watched Jesus. They watched His lifestyle and His prayer life. They noticed that everywhere He went He was successful. The disciples were astonished at His doctrine, for He taught as one that had authority, and not as the scribes. They noticed Jesus always ministered out of His overflow; He was never void of the power to heal, deliver and even raise the dead. They noticed Jesus was always moved with compassion. He never stepped out of love, even when He heard the news that His cousin, John the Baptist, had been beheaded. Instead of going to the mountain to be alone as His first reaction, He saw the multitude and was moved with compassion. He put aside His own feelings and ministered to them. He wanted to meet their needs first, therefore placing His own needs aside. Jesus always moved in wisdom and in the perfect timing of His Father's will. Not His own will, but the will of Him that sent Him. He was in tune to the unspoken needs of the people He ministered to, for the gifts of the Holy Spirit operated through him. (1 Cor. 12:8–11) Jesus never was lifted up in pride. He would say, "My Father in Me, He doeth the works". (John 14:10) He had complete confidence in His Father God so much that He knew He would be raised from the dead by the glory of the Father. Jesus demonstrated a life of prayer. There were times He prayed all night. We know he studied the Scripture, for he was full of the Word, but He never neglected His lifeline of prayer.

One day the disciples asked the golden question, 'Lord, teach us to pray.' They wanted to know how to pray the way Jesus prayed. I want you to notice they did not say, 'Lord, teach us how to prepare sermons that are homiletically correct.' They did not say, 'teach us how to operate in the gifts of the Spirit; teach us how to heal the sick and cast out demons.' They wanted to understand the art of effective prayer, therefore they said, "Lord, teach us to pray."

"So He said unto them, "When you pray, say: Our Father." I want you to notice the first principle he taught them. "When you pray," you pray to the Father; he introduces the disciples to their Father. This speaks of a relationship with the God of all creation, with you being His child. "Our Father." My Father, this is family; this is commitment, my Father.

Now we know under the New Testament we go to the Father through the name Jesus. The name of Jesus not only has power and authority over Satan and his kingdom, but also gives us access to the throne of God. All of our prayers under the New Testament are to be prayed to the Father in the name of Jesus.

> And in that day you will ask Me nothing. Most assuredly,
> I say to you, whatever you ask the Father in My name

> He will give you. Until now you have asked nothing in My name. Ask, and you will receive, that your joy may be full. (John 16:23–24)

> Jesus said to him, "I am the way, the truth, and the life. No one comes to the Father except through Me. (John 14:6)

> And whatever you ask in My name, that will I do, that the Father may be glorified in the Son. (John 14:13)

After Jesus introduces the disciples to prayer to the Father, He goes on to teach them how to receive answers to their own prayer requests. Let us call this prayer the 'prayer of faith.' We go to the Father through the name of Jesus. We have a personal need. This need may be salvation, healing, deliverance, safety, soundness or financial. In Romans 1:16, the word "salvation" in the Greek *Expository Dictionary of New Testament Words* tells us that the gospel is complete. God promises to meet all your needs according to His riches and glory. His will is His word. We find out what His will is for our individual need. We ask Him for this 'bread'. We believe we receive it and thank Him for it. We must also remember to ask God to cleanse our hearts from any sins not repented and practice forgiveness for anyone who has offended us.

> Have faith in God...what things you desire when you pray, believe you receive them, and you shall have them. And when you stand praying, forgive, if you have ought against any, that your Father also which is in heaven may forgive you your trespasses. (Mark 11:22, 24, 25)

"Which of you shall have a friend." I call this friend "the source of help", the source of supply; His name is "El Shaddai", our God who is more than enough. We are in covenant with Him. He is also our Father. We are in relationship with Him. He is God, our God. We know who He is, and we know what He promised He would do in His Word if someone would just come to Him in faith. We know He likes us to come expecting. We know He is able to do for us exceedingly and abundantly above all we could ask, hope, dream, or desire. We know He is love and He cannot fail.

I have this kind of friend and I am coming to Him with a request. This request is not for me. This request is on behalf of a friend of mine who has been put into my life for such a time as this. This friend is my responsibility; I am an intercessor for him or her. I may understand God in a more intimate way, or maybe this person has always been strong but has been going through a trial in life and needs someone to stand with them. Whatever the prayer assignment may be, it is important enough to you and to the Holy Spirit for you to go to the One who has all the answers. All the circumstances for every prayer request may be different, but certain spiritual laws remain the same. Prayer changes things. This person has come to me in a time of need on his journey in life, and I, in and of myself, have nothing to give them. But the source of help has the bread and I need it, not for myself but on their behalf. I am an intercessor and I am boldly coming to the throne of grace on behalf of my friend. I ask specifically for three loaves.

"And he from within [source of help] shall answer and say, 'Trouble me not: the door is now shut, and my children are with me in bed; I cannot rise and give thee.'" An intercessor is not moved by what he sees or hears or feels. An intercessor stands in faith on the written Word of God. His Word never fails. God hastens His Word to perform it and He does not lie. His word is forever settled in heaven. So what happened? It doesn't matter. Having done all to stand, stand therefore, unmovable, always abounding in the work of intercession, knowing that your prayers are not in vain. An intercessor never quits praying just because he sees no visible results. (Luke 18:1) It may look like your prayers are not working. It may take days, it may take months, or it may take years. Your intercession for that particular need is working. Oftentimes things in the natural become worse before they get better. The reason for these manifestations is because your prayers are stirring things up in the spiritual realm, and the devil doesn't like it. He has been in charge in that area for a long time and does not want to give up easily. He is stubborn. Show him just how patient you can be and he will give up his stronghold. Another reason things may become worse is because at times, the person you are praying for is stubborn and does not want to give into the promptings of the Holy Spirit. He may be a Christian that is walking in some area of disobedience. Do not become discouraged; eventually every knee must bow and every tongue must confess that Jesus Christ is Lord.

"Though he will not rise and give him, because he is his friend, yet because of his importunity he will rise and give him as many as he needeth." This man is the intercessor's friend. He comes to the door at an unreasonable hour of the night. He knew he could, because they were friends. The intercessor knew that his friend would "in no wise cast him out," but that is not why he received the answer to his request. The intercessor had an urgent request and needed a direct response. So at this moment, based on 'importunity,' the source of help rose up and gave the intercessor not just three loaves, but as many as he needed.

Why did this intercessor receive the help necessary for his friend? The scripture says because of his importunity. Webster's dictionary defines the word importunity as 'the state or quality of being importunate; persistence in solicitation.' Webster's also defines solicitation as 'entreaty, urging, or importunity; a petition or request.' The prayer of intercession is a different form of prayer compared to the prayer of faith. When praying the prayer of faith, you are praying for yourself, for your own needs to be met; you believe you receive and thank God for the answer. The prayer of intercession is made on the behalf of another. The intercessor knows God, and knows who he is in Christ Jesus. He boldly goes to the throne of grace in order to bring spiritual, physical or emotional help for someone in need. Because of this intercessors love, faith and persistence, he is able to accomplish success in prayer on behalf of this person.

The intercessor's reward is from God, and it does not matter to him if his friend at home knows who labored in prayer for him. The only thing that matters is that God sees and He has promised to reward the intercessor. Hebrews 6:10 tells us that God is not unrighteous to forget your work and labor of love. You are laying up treasures in heaven. These labors will follow you and great will be your reward.

> Therefore, my beloved brethren, be steadfast, immovable, always abounding in the work of the Lord, knowing that your labor is not in vain in the Lord. (1 Cor. 15:58)

What is an Intercessor?

Chapter 9

So I sought for a man among them who would make a wall, and stand in the gap before Me on behalf of the land, that I should not destroy it; but I found no one. (Ezek. 22:30)

An intercessor is one who stands in the gap as a mediator. The mediator's purpose or function is to bring agreement. An intercessor is one who takes the place of another. In the scripture above we read that God is literally searching for someone to intercede. In the context of this scripture, He is looking for someone to stand in the gap for the land so that the land would not be destroyed. God is still searching for intercessors today.

> For he is not a man, as I am, that I should answer Him, And that we should go to court together. Nor is there any mediator between us, who may lay his hand on us both. (Job 9:32, 33)

Job saw his need for an intercessor. He is saying that he needed someone to lay one hand on himself and one hand on God. This is what an intercessor does; he acts as a lawyer and pleads the case of the person for whom he is praying. The case is being pleaded before the throne of grace with the book of the law, the Word of God. God is looking for someone to help the lost soul, a hurting individual, a city or a nation taken captive by unrighteousness. His will is that all men be saved and come to the knowledge of the truth. When we pray, we release the will of God on the earth. We untie the hands of God so that He can do what he desires to do in the earth. 'Thy will be done on earth as it is in heaven.' We have not because we ask not. (James 4:2) Ask for the heathen; they are our inheritance (Ps. 2:8) Man is God's avenue into the earth; God and man have always worked together. God has a plan, but because Satan is the god of this world, He needs us to work with Him. He needs permission in order to execute His will. Our prayers avail much. (James 5:16) We are the men and women that can pray and change things. Again, you as an intercessor lay one hand on man and one hand on God. You are the mediator; you are the go-between. An intercessor grabs hold of the person in prayer and holds onto him, while holding onto God at the same time. The intercessor then begins to ask of God. He reminds God of His goodness and mercy. He quotes the scripture that is appropriate for the individual that is the subject of prayer. While in this place of prayer, use your spiritual imagination. Visualize yourself literally laying your hand on that person and your other hand on God. Visualizing will help keep your flow and your focus. While in prayer, your mind can tend to wander. Visualization is a powerful tool that will train your mind to be kept in the right place. (Isa. 26:3)

> For then you will have your delight in the Almighty, And lift up your face to God. You will make your prayer to Him, He will hear you, And you will pay your vows. You will also declare a thing, And it will be established for you; So light will shine on your ways. When they cast you down, and you say, 'Exaltation will come!' Then He will save the humble person. He will even deliver the one who is not innocent; Yes, he will be delivered by the purity of your hands. (Job 22:26–30)

As a born again believer, you are what the Bible calls "the righteousness of God in Christ Jesus". You are in right standing with God because of the new birth. "He [Jesus] who knew no sin became sin for us that we might be made the righteousness of God in Christ Jesus." (2 Cor. 5:21) "There is therefore no condemnation to those who are in Christ."

(Rom. 8:1) You are clean through the Word of God. You are guiltless and free from the penalty of sin. Jesus took care of sin at the cross. "You are washed, you are sanctified, and you are justified." (1 Cor. 6:11) This means *just as if you never sinned.* Now if you do sin, you have an advocate with the Father, an intercessor: Jesus! You go to God in the name of Jesus and ask for forgiveness. You are again in right standing with God. (1 John 1:9) It is important to establish this fact, because this knowledge reinforces your confidence and boldness before the throne of God.

Notice the scripture says, "He will deliver the one who is not innocent; yes, he will be delivered by the purity of your hands." Your hands are clean because of Jesus. You have that revelation. Now your intercessions on behalf of someone who is guilty will help to deliver them. 'They will be delivered because of the pureness of your hands.' There are some people who will never be saved, healed or delivered from trouble unless someone prays for them. You are laying one hand on man and one hand on God. Deliverance will come because of the cleanness of your hands. God honors your prayers, God honors His Word, and God honors the covenant He has with you. Hold on to that person. Don't let go; pray with importunity.

> Keep yourself in the love of God, looking for the mercy of our Lord Jesus Christ unto eternal life. And on some have compassion, making a distinction; but others save with fear, pulling them out of the fire, hating even the garment defiled by the flesh. (Jude 1:21–23)

First of all, this scripture begins with the commandment to keep yourself in the love of God. As stated earlier, the love of God is the motivation for all our prayers. If you are having a difficult time walking in love toward an individual, pray for them! You will begin to see them through the eyes of God. What you see will affect your heart, your attitudes, your behavior toward that person, and, in time, your emotions or feelings. Keep yourself in the love of God. As you enter into intercession for an individual, you are laying one hand on them and one hand on God. Through the spiritual force of love and faith as well as your persistence, you are pulling them toward the light of God's truth instead of the spiritual darkness and then ultimately eternal damnation. If this person has knowingly or unknowingly rejected Jesus, he or she is not born–again and therefore not going into heaven. Unfortunately they are hell bound for all of eternity. The Bible speaks of 'the lake of fire,' or 'the abyss'. (Rev. 20:10) The Bible also speaks of 'the everlasting fire and eternal punishment'. (Matt. 25:41–46) We also have the example of the rich man and Lazarus in Luke 16:22–26. Hell is a real place; so is heaven. God's will is that all men be saved and come to the knowledge of the truth. He also said in Psalms 2:8, "Ask of Me, and I will give You The nations for Your inheritance, and the ends of the earth for Your possession."

We are not always allowed to see what is happening in intercession; therefore we must abide in the spirit and walk by faith. There are times when the gifts of the Spirit will sovereignly operate during your prayer time. As He wills, He may choose to reveal to you through not just an inward knowing or a 'witness' in your heart, but possibly through vision. We need not be afraid of the supernatural. We are to desire these manifestations, but if they don't come, do not be affected in your faith. When they do come, they are encouraging not only to you but to the Body of Christ. I remember one time before a speaking engagement, three others and myself were in a time of intercession on behalf of the lost. The anointing to pray was particularly strong that afternoon. After yielding to the Holy Spirit, I went into a deeper place of prayer where I was more conscious of spiritual things than natural things. As we continued in prayer I saw a big hole filled with darkness. This hole had a force like a vacuum whereby it was pulling people into it. No matter how hard the people waved their arms and legs, they were hopelessly at the mercy of this force pulling them into eternal damnation. This scripture came to me: "multitudes and multitudes in the valley of decision". (Joel 3:14) What I saw affected my heart. I began to pray for these people. I asked God for mercy on their behalf. I began to cry. I was not worshipping God or praying the prayer of faith. This was true intercession at a deeper level. I felt incredible compassion for the people. As this compassion rose up from within, I cried tears for them. I again asked God for mercy. My heart felt as if it were being torn. All my attention: spirit, soul and body were on God and praying through to help on behalf of these people. I reminded God of His word, but mostly prayed in tongues and cried. The deepest part of me was calling and meeting with the deepest part of God. I felt toil, labor, and sadness. The people that were praying with me hooked up with me in prayer and entered in. As we were praying, the descent into this hole was stopped for some, and for others the decent slowed down considerably. We had one hand on God and one hand on the people for whom we were in intercession. I know our prayers availed much. Who were we praying for? Were they the unsaved in attendance at the church meeting that night? Were we praying for individuals in another city or nation? I don't know. We know in part and prophesy in part. Thank God for the part we do know. Our prayers had availed much on behalf of individuals who needed salvation. We interceded for sometime until we felt what I call a release. There was joy and peace. We had completed our prayer assignment for that evening.

> And the Lord restored Job's losses when he prayed for his friends. Indeed the Lord gave Job twice as much as he had before. (Job 42:10)

An intercessor is a blessed man or woman. When you stand in the gap on behalf of someone, you are setting certain spiritual laws in motion on your behalf as well. You are operating in the law of love under the New Testament. As a result, expect the blessings found in Deuteronomy 28 to come upon you and overtake you. When Job prayed for his friends, God not only took care of Jobs captivity, but also blessed him with twice as much as he had before. You can apply this scripture to your own life as well. What is your captivity? What needs do you have? It is more blessed to give than it is to receive. When you sow prayer, not only will you reap prayer for your needs, but God will bless you exceedingly and abundantly above all you could ask, hope, dream, or desire.

The Priority of Prayer

Chapter 10

Therefore I exhort first of all that supplications, prayers, intercessions, and giving of thanks be made for all men, for kings and all who are in authority, that we may lead a quiet and peaceable life in all godliness and reverence. For this is good and acceptable in the sight of God our Savior, who desires all men to be saved and to come to the knowledge of the truth. (1 Tim. 2:1–4)

God has priorities. He has reasons for His priorities. The above scripture is an exhortation for us to keep our priorities the same as Gods' priorities. First, before you pray for anything else, pray for your leaders. This includes the leaders on a national, state, provincial and city level. I am writing this chapter with the nation of America in mind, but this can apply to any nation as well. God said, "first of all, supplications, intercessions, prayers, and giving of thanks, be made for all men; for kings, and for all that are in authority." Why did He say that? "That we may lead a quiet and peaceable life in all godliness and honesty." It does not matter if the leaders are born–again or not. We are to pray for them; it will benefit our nation and ultimately affect us.

The Christians are the ones with authority in this land. This authority carries with it major responsibility. We are responsible for what is happening on our homeland. God will hold us accountable. God's desire is that we lead a quiet and peaceable life. His will is not wars. (John 10:10) His will is not financial lack. (Phil. 4:19) His will is not that we live in fear of terrorist attacks. His will is not that other countries have weapons of mass destruction and that our nation be in the dark. His will is peace. We must therefore obey the scripture and pray for our nation, or we are in sin. (1 Sam. 12:23)

To whom much is given, much is required. This nation has been given much in the way of Gospel teaching. We are required by God to pray that His will would be done on earth as it is in heaven. There is peace and harmony in heaven. We have not because we ask not.

> So I sought for a man among them who would make a wall, and stand in the gap before Me on behalf of the land, that I should not destroy it; but I found no one. Therefore I have poured out My indignation on them; I have consumed them with the fire of My wrath; and I have recompensed their deeds on their own heads," says the Lord God. (Ez. 22:30–31)

In this particular scripture, God is speaking to a nation. He said if He could find one man who would stand in the gap, judgment would not have come. Just one! Imagine if He found two. "One will put a thousand to flight; two will put ten thousand to flight." As stated earlier, Satan is the god of this present age. We must exercise authority over him so that Gods' plans and purposes are fulfilled in our nation. God can only intervene as intercessors seek His face and ask Him to move.

> If my people, who are called by my name, will humble themselves and pray and seek my face, and turn from their wicked ways, then I will hear from heaven, and will forgive their sin and heal their land. (2 Chron. 7:14)

The church needs to wake up and realize that we have an enemy. Let us not just look in the natural realm and discuss at a conference table who they are. We have an enemy in the unseen realm. There are spirits of darkness whose primary attack is against our nation and all it stands for. Whatever has manifested in this natural realm has had its origin in the spirit realm first. We can abort the enemy's plans through persistent intercession on behalf of our country. We must not be ignorant of Satan's devices. Your prayers are effective and you are able to effect change in this nation by what is done privately in the prayer closet. We must not sit by and think, 'well it was prophesied that all these things would come in the last days.' No! We will arise and we will take our place. Abraham is an example of an intercessor that stood in the gap for two cities: Sodom and Gomorrah. He was a man who took his place in prayer.

> And the Lord God said, "Shall I hide from Abraham what I am about to do, since Abraham shall surely become a great and mighty nation, and in him all the nations of the earth will be blessed? For I have chosen him, in order that he may command his children and his household after him to keep the way of the Lord by doing righteousness and justice; in order that the Lord may bring upon Abraham what He has spoken about him." And the Lord said, "the outcry against Sodom and Gomorrah is great, and because their sin is very grave I will go down now and see whether they have done altogether according to the outcry against it that has come to Me; and if not, I will know." (Gen. 18:17–21) (NASB)

The Lord said, "Shall I hide from Abraham what I am about to do?" That is a powerful statement. Why did God ask that question? Who was Abraham? My friend, he was in covenant with God. They had an agreement. In order for God to do what He desired, He needed Abraham's permission. God needed legal permission. He could not destroy those wicked cities without informing Abraham. Additionally, God said, "For I have known him". God knew that Abraham would continue his part of the covenant and remain a man of integrity.

As New Testament believers, we are under a better covenant based upon better promises. (Heb. 8:6) Through the blood of Jesus Christ, we are also known by our Heavenly Father. We stand complete in Him, pure and holy before the throne of God. This scripture is relative to the time we live in now. Our prayers are just as relevant and effective as Abraham's. Let us see what happens next.

> Then the men turned away from there and went toward Sodom, but Abraham stood before the Lord. Abraham drew near and said, "would you also destroy the righteous with the wicked? Suppose there were fifty righteous within the city; would you also destroy the place and not spare it for the fifty righteous that were in it? Far be it from You to do such a thing as this, to slay the righteous with the wicked; far be it from You! Shall not the Judge of all the earth do right? So the Lord said, "if I find in Sodom fifty righteous within the city, then I will spare all the place for their sakes." (Gen. 18:22–26)

Abraham drew near and stood before the Lord. He stood in faith. He was not afraid. Abraham knew who God was. He knew that God is a God of mercy, love and forgiveness. He also approached God based on his covenant with Him. Today, we can do the same. Hebrews 4:16 says, "Let us therefore come boldly to the throne of grace, that we may obtain mercy and find grace to help in time of need." It also says in James 4:8, "Draw near to God and He will draw near to you." Where sin abounds, grace does so much the more abound. We are able under the New Testament to go to God on behalf of our nation and ask Him for mercy; ask Him for a spirit of revival; ask Him to open up the "eyes of our understanding" so that our nation can return to our first love. Jesus is the Way, the Truth, and the Life this nation needs. We have not because we ask not. Abraham's request was that if there were fifty righteous, the city would be spared. God said yes, He would spare the city for the sake of fifty. Abraham kept going down in number until he said, "Suppose ten should be found there." And the Lord said, "I will not destroy it for the sake of ten." Abraham's prayers availed much. So do your prayers.

We have more than ten righteous in our nation today! American Christians, take your place. Be confident in the prayers you are setting yourself to pray. When you have run out of Scripture to pray, pray in tongues. God knows the needs of this nation and knows how to get the needs accomplished. He knows the plots that are being drawn up by our enemy. Pray that everything hidden will be revealed. Pray for divine protection on our borders. Pray for wisdom for the leaders of this nation. "Now My eyes will be open and My ears attentive unto the prayers that are made for your nation. I will forgive your sin and heal your land."

How to Pray the Prayer of Intercession

Chapter 11

For if I pray in a tongue, my spirit prays, but my understanding is unfruitful. What is the conclusion then? I will pray with the spirit, I will also pray with the understanding.
(1 Cor. 14:14–15)

The scripture says, "I will pray." Many times you simply set yourself to pray for that individual. By natural knowledge you may be aware of their needs; maybe they even asked you to pray for them. There are other times that you may not even know they have a need. Maybe they did not ask you to pray, but you may at times have what I call a 'burden' for them. You think of them often that day or that week; you are troubled in your spirit for them and don't know why. You have a 'love' for them. These are the times the Holy Spirit knows their needs, and because you are a friend or relative or just because you have made yourself available to be an intercessor, God will search you out and desire to use you as a vessel of prayer on their behalf. No matter how the prayer request comes, either by natural or supernatural knowledge, your will is involved. It is your choice as to whether or not you stir yourself up to pray on their behalf.

The apostle Paul said, "I will pray with the spirit, I will pray with the understanding also." There are two ways to pray the prayer of intercession on the first level: in your known language and in tongues. When praying in your known language, remember this: do not pray the problem. God knows the problem; more importantly, He has the answer. All the answers you need on their behalf are found in the Word of God. Pray the Word of God. Take their need to the Word. Agree with the Word, not the problem. Now lay one hand on them and one hand on God. Present the promises found in His Word before the throne of God.

> So shall My word be that goes forth from My mouth; It shall not return to Me void, But it shall accomplish what I please, And it shall prosper in the thing for which I sent it. (Isa. 55:11)

> For I am ready to perform My word. (Jer. 1:12)

> He sent His word and healed them, and delivered them from their destructions. (Ps. 107:20)

> Speak the word only, and my servant will be healed. (Matt. 8:8)

After you have prayed all you know to pray in your understanding, now pray in tongues. "He that speaks in an unknown tongue speaks not unto men but unto God." (1 Cor. 14:2) The Holy Spirit knows exactly what to pray for. As you intercede in tongues, you are speaking to God on behalf of that person. When you are praying in tongues, you are praying the will of God. You are praying with the help of the Holy Spirit who knows all things. You are praying with His ability.

He may not reveal all you are praying about, for He is a gentleman and will not reveal the secrets of men's hearts. You must trust the intercession of the Holy Spirit as you yield to Him in tongues.

We may see a person's need and agree with the Word for their need. We may receive a prayer request from a person, but they may not be telling you all about the circumstances. There is not anything hidden from the Holy Spirit. He knows exactly what is in the heart of a person. He knows who is influencing that person. The Holy Spirit knows all. Tongues, for the intercessor, is an amazing tool for answered prayer. After I pray the Word of God, I do a majority of my intercessions in other tongues. I do not know exactly what to pray. Thank God for the precious Holy Spirit;

He is our Helper. He is called alongside to help us when we have prayed all we know to pray.

> So too the Holy Spirit comes to our aid and bears us up in our weakness; for we do not know what prayer to offer nor how to offer worthily as we ought, but the Spirit Himself goes to meet our supplication and pleads in our behalf with unspeakable yearnings and groanings too deep for utterance. And He who searches the hearts of men knows what is in the mind of the [Holy] Spirit [what His intent is], because the Spirit intercedes and pleads [before God] in behalf of the saints according to and in harmony with God's will. We are assured and know that [God being a partner in their labor] all things work together and are [fitting into a plan] for good to and for those who love God and are called according to [His] design and purpose. (Rom. 8:26–28) (AMP)

Never pray your will or your desires on behalf of a person. Always pray the Word of God and in tongues. Praying your will, thoughts or desires on a person is unscriptural and ungodly. You are imposing your will on them, not the will of God. This type of 'prayer' is a form of witchcraft. For example, let's say you have a single Christian friend who asked you to pray that God would send him or her a lifelong mate. We know that it is God's will for a man and a woman not to be alone. (Gen. 2:18) As you stand to pray for them, you remind God of His word regarding marriage. Next, just begin to pray in tongues for them! Don't play God and become involved with who the person might be or what kind of person you think they belong with! God may use you to help connect them with a Christian person from church or at work, but don't become involved with outward appearance and pray that God would hook them up with a particular person. They might not be compatible and it might not be God's will for their lives. Pray the Word of God and pray in tongues. The Lord will lead, guide, and direct the path of the person for whom you are in intercession.

Now may the God of peace Himself sanctify you completely; and may your whole spirit, soul, and body be preserved blameless at the coming of the Lord Jesus Christ. (1 Thess. 5:23)

When you pray in tongues or in the spirit, you are communicating with your Heavenly Father. He understands you. This is your spirit man talking with the Father of spirits. Tongues are a direct hotline to Heaven. When you pray in the spirit, you are praying out the mind, will, and purposes of God. You are praying in line with God's purposes and timing. You are praying the government of God. What is His will? What is His purpose? My friend, His will and purposes are found in His Word. You are praying according to His Word.

We must trust the ministry of the Holy Spirit as it relates to prayer. He knows the needs and He knows how to accurately pray. He helps our infirmity. The word 'infirmity' in the Greek means 'our inability to produce results'. We do not always know what the entire situation is surrounding a matter for which we are in intercession. The Holy Spirit knows all. We must go beyond what we know and enter into intercession and pray in tongues. He knows exactly what to pray! He does not miss the target. As we do this, we will see amazing results in our prayers.

Scripture Prayers For The Believer

Chapter 12

Pray (also) for one another that you may be healed and restored (to a spiritual tone of mind and heart). The earnest (heartfelt, continued) prayer of a righteous man makes tremendous power available (dynamic in its working).

(James 5:16) (AMP)

When I am asked to pray for a person, the first thing I need to know is are they a believer or are they a nonbeliever. If they are a believer, they are alive unto God. They are the temples of the Holy Spirit. "Do you not know that you are the temple of God and that the Spirit of God dwells in you?" (1 Cor. 3:16, 6:19; 2 Cor. 6:16; Eph. 2:22) If they are a believer, God lives in them and works from within that person, as well as form the outside. They may be a believer that is in some type of sin or are bound by a habit, or a new Christian that is having trouble understanding the scriptures or is bound by sickness. Whatever their problem is, there is scripture found in the Word of God that is available to pray, and get results.

You are an intercessor. A person comes to you with a need. Or maybe their name came up in a prayer meeting. Maybe you had a dream in the night for this person and the Holy Spirit gave you a word of knowledge or a word of wisdom about their particular situation. However their need is presented to you, you have the power in prayer. You know what the Word of God has to say about the problem and you know how to apply it. As stated in a previous chapter, while in intercession on the first level, you lay one hand on God and one hand on the person. You are the mediator; you are the go–between. You are as a lawyer who pleads their case with the Word of God as your foundation. You then take their need to the Word and agree with the Word of God, and that is what you present before the throne of grace. (Heb. 4:16) Pray the answer to their need, not the problem. Let's say that the person is having trouble understanding God's love for them. They have fruits of fear and insecurity. They are condemned all the time or may have trouble holding onto relationships. Maybe they just suffered the loss of a loved one through death or divorce. They truly need a revelation of the Agape (love) of God for them. God is love, as found in 1 Corinthians 13:4–8 and 1 John 4:16. This divine enlightenment or revelation will set them free from fear, insecurity and even depression. (John 8:32)

> There is no fear in love; but perfect love casts out fear,
> because fear involves torment. But he who fears has not
> been made perfect in love. (1 John 4:18)

As a result of their lack of knowledge of the love of God for them, they are perishing. (Hosea 4:6) You, at this point in your walk with God, have come through maybe the same trial of unbelief and are now able to help this person, not in a counseling session, but in a private session of prayer. How do you pray? What can you give them?

> We then that are strong ought to bear the infirmities of
> the weak, and not to please ourselves. (Rom. 15:1) (KJV)

The word "bear" means to lift up with the idea of removing. The word "infirmities" in this scripture means "a scruple of conscience". This is not speaking of a physical thing, but it is speaking of something wrong in their belief. Through your intercessions, you are lifting up with the idea of removing wrong or negative thinking that has kept them bound by Satan's strongholds, and lack of revelation of the Word of God in their particular situation. This particular person needs a revelation of the love of God, as well as strength in their inner man so that they can rise up in victory as more than a conqueror. (Rom. 8:37) Pray that they will be strengthened in their inner man and pray that they would have a revelation of the love of God. Insert their name in the following scripture and then pray in tongues.

> For this reason I bow my knees to the Father of our Lord Jesus Christ, from whom the whole family in heaven and earth is named, that He would grant you according to the riches of His glory, to be strengthened with might through His Spirit in the inner man, that Christ may dwell in your hearts through faith, that you, being rooted and grounded in love, may be able to comprehend with all saints what is the width and length and depth and height, to know the love of Christ which passes knowledge; that you may be filled with all the fullness of God. (Eph. 3:14–19)

You have a Bible full of verses that can be used in intercession on behalf of a person and their particular need. Here is another scripture you can pray for a believer that is in need of personal direction or wisdom in dealing with any challenge that life brings.

> For this reason we also, since the day we heard it, do not cease to pray for you, and to ask that you may be filled with the knowledge of His will in all wisdom and spiritual understanding. (Col. 1:9)

Notice that the apostle Paul said, 'we do not cease to pray for you'. These Holy Spirit–inspired prayers can be prayed over and over on behalf of a person and even for yourself. The will of God is found in the Word of God. God has given us His written Word, and through His Word the will of God can be found. Yes, the Holy Spirit leads and guides us through other means (for example, the inner witness or the voice of our conscience), but primarily He speaks through His Word. I have had many times in my walk with God whereby certain scriptures seemed to 'light up,' and God spoke a *rhema* to my heart. I have also had countless times whereby I was praying or just doing nothing 'spiritual' and a scripture rose up in my heart. I had to look it up and find the exact reference and

God was able to lead, guide or even comfort me personally through His Word. This too can happen for the person for whom you are praying.

The psalmist David said, "Your word is a lamp unto my feet and a light to my path." (Ps. 119:105) Here is another scripture you can pray for a believer who may be in a spiritually dry time in their walk with God or may be having a hard time understanding the Scriptures.

> I do not cease to give thanks for you, making mention of you in my prayers: that the God of our Lord Jesus Christ, the Father of glory, may give to you the spirit of wisdom and revelation in the knowledge of Him, the eyes of your understanding being enlightened; that you may know what is the hope of His calling, what are the riches of the glory of His inheritance in the saints. (Eph. 1:16–18)

Your spirit man has eyes. A believer needs to perceive with His spirit man what is the truth found in the Word of God. The more revelation one has in the Scriptures, the more he is able to walk in the light of life found only in Jesus. Believers must overcome dullness of perception as it relates to the things of God. Praying these prayers will produce enlightenment.

And He opened their understanding, that they might comprehend the Scriptures. (Luke 24:45)

> Therefore we also, since we are surrounded by so great a cloud of witnesses, let us lay aside every weight, and the sin which so easily ensnares us, and let us run with endurance the race that is set before us, looking unto Jesus, the author and finisher of our faith, who for the joy that was set before Him endured the cross, despising the shame, and has sat down at the right hand of the throne of God. (Heb. 12:1, 2)

As Christians, we are running in a spiritual race. Some are having a hard time with weights and sins. These weights are wrapped around them and are slowing them down. They are falling because of sin. Some are even having a hard time getting back up. They may even be carrying heavy burdens from hurts brought on by people from the past. They may have faults or sins in their lives that they are having trouble getting rid of. These are all hindrances that are keeping them from running a successful race. Intercession on their behalf can help lift these burdens.

> Bear one another's burdens, and so fulfill the law of Christ. (Gal. 6:2)

Instead of judging and criticizing another believer for weights and sin they may be carrying, we should be fulfilling the royal law of love by praying for them. Matthew 7:1–2 says, "Judge not, that you be not judged. For with what judgment you judge, you will be judged; and with the measure you use, it will be measured back to you." Jesus died for their sins: past, present, and future. We then that are strong ought to bear the infirmity of the weak. That word 'bear' means to lift up with the idea of completely removing. Intercession is involved in bearing one another's burdens. In the spirit, you are lifting off of them the weight and sins that keep them from a successful Christian walk. When we all take our place in intercession for one another, we are helping the entire body of Christ come into a place of maturity.

> Simon, Simon! Satan has asked for you, that he may sift you as wheat. But I have prayed for you; that your faith should not fail; and when you have returned to Me, strengthen your brethren. (Luke 22:31, 32)

There are times when, as an intercessor, you must take authority over the works of demon activity that may be at work in the life of a believer. A believer cannot be demon possessed, but they can be demon oppressed. Sin in the life of a believer opens up the door for demon activity. Ignorance or self-pity can open up the door to the devil. Sometimes you may be dealing with a believer who is weak in the faith and needs prayer support. Every circumstance is different. You, as an intercessor, can use the name of Jesus on their behalf and loose them from these strongholds. They have their own authority, but depending on their situation, they are not using it. They may be tired spiritually, or worn out mentally and physically. You are the one who is strong; command the devil to leave!

Intercession For The Unbeliever

Chapter 13

But even if our gospel is veiled, it is veiled to those who are perishing, whose minds the god of this age has blinded, who do not believe, lest the light of the gospel of the glory of Christ, who is the image of God, should shine on them.

(2 Cor. 4:3, 4)

*T*his scripture is speaking of people who have never accepted Jesus Christ as their own personal Savior. This scripture does not speak of joining a church or denomination as we know today. This is a personal salvation between an individual and God– not any god. This scripture speaks of the one true God, the Father of the Lord Jesus Christ who died on a cross at Calvary. Sin came in through man, and redemption came through the man, Jesus Christ. (1 Cor. 15:22, 23) He was the "Lamb that was slain to take away the sins of the world." (Rev. 13:8) There are many false prophets that have gone out into the world. 1 John 4:1, 2 says, "Beloved, do not believe every spirit, but test the spirits, whether they are of God; because many false prophets have gone out into the world. By this you know the Spirit of God, every spirit that confesses that Jesus Christ has come in the flesh is of God." If a man or woman does not acknowledge Jesus Christ as their Lord, they are not what the bible calls "born again". Their spirit is not alive unto God; they are spiritually dead and on their way to hell for all of eternity. They are lost. They are separated from God. Jesus said, "They are of their father the devil". (John 8:44)

Most assuredly, I say to you, unless one is born again, he cannot see the kingdom of God. Most assuredly, I say to you, unless one is born of water and the Spirit, he cannot enter the kingdom of God. That which is born of the flesh is flesh, and that which is born of the Spirit is spirit. John 3:3,5–6

To the unbeliever, the gospel is veiled or hidden. They have no illumination of the Truth. "I am the Way, the Truth, and the Life. No one comes to the Father except through Me." (John 14:6) Their minds are blinded to spiritual reality. The world is hungry for spiritual things. They are looking for it, but the true reality is only found in Jesus.

When it comes to intercession for the lost, the first thing we must do is use our authority in prayer. Take authority over the devil on their behalf. John 14:14 says, "If you shall ask anything in My name, I will do it." The word "ask" here means "demand". You demand that Satan release that person in the name of Jesus! You use your authority in the name of Jesus for them because they have no authority of their own in the spirit world. They have been walking according to the course of this world; according to the prince of the power of the air, the spirit who now works in the children of disobedience. (Eph. 2:2) See yourself laying one hand on them and one hand on God. As you continue, steadfast and unmovable, in persistent intercession, you will be pulling them out of spiritual darkness and therefore pulling them toward the kingdom of light found in Jesus, snatched from the fire in Jesus' name!

[Strive to] save others, snatching [them] out of [the] fire; on others take pity [but] with fear, loathing even the garment spotted by the flesh and polluted by their sensuality. (Jude 1:23) (AMP)

As you spend time in prayer for the unsaved, you are preparing the way for them to be born again. You are tilling the ground of their heart. The name of Jesus, used on their behalf, is releasing them from strongholds that are influencing their mind. I would also suggest that you pray Psalm 91 on their behalf. Make this Psalm personal by inserting their name within the scripture text. This is the Psalm of protection. As you, the intercessor, are praying, angels are released on their behalf. They will protect the one for whom you are praying. (Heb. 1:14; Ps. 103:20)

Intercession on behalf of the unbeliever will also release the conviction of the Holy Spirit.

> Nevertheless I tell you the truth. It is to your advantage that I go away; for if I do not go away, the Helper will not come to you; but if I depart, I will send Him to you. And when He has come, he will convict the world of sin, and of righteousness and of judgment: of sin because they do not believe in Me; of righteousness, because I go to My Father and you see Me no more; of judgment, because the ruler of this world is judged. (John 16:7–11)

The only sin the unbeliever is guilty of is rejecting Jesus. This is the sin nature that separates man from God. Jesus is the way back into fellowship with the Father God. We are talking about a spiritual rebirth, where the old nature passes away and a new nature is born. (2 Cor. 5:17–19; Ezek. 11:19)

Oftentimes, when an intercessor begins to target a person through prayer, the manifestations of darkness may get worse before they get better. You may ask why? First of all, if they are an unbeliever, they are becoming increasingly unhappy with what they don't have in Christ, but we know that Jesus is the only way, truth, and life. They are being convicted by the Holy Spirit and He is drawing them away form the comforts or pleasures of this world and drawing them to salvation through Jesus Christ. There may also be demonic activity influencing them that is fighting for dominion over that individual that does not want to give up without a fight. Remember, you are fighting for his or her salvation, so do not quit praying. If things are becoming worse in the natural, "seen" realm, it is because you are making progress in the unseen spirit realm. Do not look at the outward appearance! Never judge the success of your prayers on outward appearance. You must abide in faith and not waiver. (James 1:6–8)

> Men ought to always pray and not lose heart. (Luke 18:1) (KJV)

> Therefore, my beloved brethren, be steadfast, immovable, always abounding in the work of the Lord, knowing that your labor is not in vain in the Lord. (1 Cor. 15:58)

Intercession is hard work and it is a labor of love. Don't quit or faint if you don't see visible results. That is exactly what the enemy wants you to do. Discouragement is the number one reason for prayer defeats. You must be stubborn in the spirit! You must be strong in the Lord and in the power of His might and unconditional love! Love never fails and neither will you, if you remain faithful and persistent in asking of God and demanding of Satan on behalf of those for whom you are interceding.

Romans 10:13–15 says, "For whosoever calls on the name of the Lord shall be saved. How then shall they call on Him in whom they have not believed? And how shall they believe in Him in whom they have not heard? And how shall they hear without a preacher? And how shall they preach unless they are sent? As it is written: How beautiful are the feet of those who preach the gospel of peace, who bring glad tidings of good things!" Pray for a Christian to come across the path of the person you are praying for. Ask God to do it and He will.

> Therefore pray the Lord of the harvest to send out laborers into His harvest. (Matt. 9:38)

Faith comes by hearing and hearing the Word of God. (Rom. 10:17) Every person has faith to be saved. (Rom. 12:13) Pray for a 'laborer' to come across the path of the unsaved person, someone to whom this person can relate in the natural sense. For example, if you are praying for your mate and he or she is successful in business, pray that someone to whom he or she can relate would be that witness! The Bible says that he that wins souls is wise! (Prov. 11:30) When a laborer comes across an unsaved person's path, that person's heart will hear truth and eventually he or she will respond. If you are consistent in prayer for this family member, oftentimes it is better for God to use someone else to speak His message to him or her. What you can do is stand on the promise found in Acts 16:31, that your entire household will be saved. Pray in secret for relatives and allow God to open the door of opportunity for someone else to speak the Word of God to them. Sometimes a stranger is better suited in reaching an unsaved family member.

Prayer for your Enemies

Chapter 14

But I say to you who hear: Love your enemies, do good to those who hate you, bless those who curse you, and pray for those who spitefully use you... But love your enemies, do good, and lend, hoping for nothing in return; and your reward will be great, and you will be sons of the Most High. For He is kind to the unthankful and evil. Therefore be merciful, just as your Father also is merciful. Judge not, and you shall not be judged. Condemn not, and you shall not be condemned. Forgive, and you will be forgiven.
(Luke 6:27, 28; 35–37)

Intercession is not prayer for yourself; it is prayer made on behalf of another. As stated earlier, this type of prayer is the greatest act of love you can do for anyone. Jesus did it, and so can you. Prayer for your enemies is probably the most challenging to any intercessor. Operating in this aspect of intercession requires walking in the commandment of love. It is complete death of human reasoning, feelings and emotions. It is walking as Jesus walked; instead of retaliating in the flesh against those who have hurt you, you are responding in the spirit. Agape love is the unconditional love of God. Agape is a powerful force in the unseen realm. The power of God is released through the love of God. By an act of your will, you can choose to love the one who has hurt you. Maybe this person falsely accused you or slandered you. Maybe you were abused physically or emotionally—maybe both. Whatever hurt was inflicted you have a choice. Are you going to let it go and forgive, or are you going to hold onto this offense? You are born of God therefore you are born of Agape Love. This type of love is not born out of your emotional realm; it is born in your human spirit. Your human spirit is the part of you that is connected to God. You have the ability to love your enemies. You know who they are, and as you read this your mind kicks in and says "What? Love who?". The Holy Spirit brings to your remembrance all things, even those you need to forgive. It does not matter who was right and who was wrong; what matters is having a pure heart of love so you can grow and be all that God has called you to be in the earth. What matters is hearing God say in that day you stand before Him, "well done, good and faithful servant". What matters is that there is nothing between you and your God. Unforgivingness will hinder your prayer life. Simply stated, God won't hear you.

> If I regard iniquity in my heart, the Lord will not hear me. (Ps. 66:18)

Prayer for your enemies is forgiveness in action. By an act of our own will, you say "God I am obeying the scripture even though I don't feel like it". Most of the time the people that hurt us the most are people we have known well. It may be a relative, like a parent or brother or sister. It may be a husband, wife, or an ex–husband or ex–wife. It may even be those we served or who served us; Jesus had that experience. He had many accusers attacking His life and ministry. Many things were said about Him that were untrue. They said He was gluttonous, a winebibber, and a friend of publicans and sinners. Many things were said about John the Baptist. People said John was a demon possessed. (Matt. 11:18–19) All Jesus did was go about doing good, healing all that were oppressed by the devil. He was misunderstood, yet He never retaliated against His enemies who were speaking evil of Him. He only sought to please the Father. He knew He had to keep His focus and fulfill His destiny. If He had listened to all of His accusers and what they were saying, He might have opened His mind and allowed seeds of doubt to enter His heart. He kept His focus on what the Father spoke of Him. He knew who He was. He was what He was by the grace given to Him by His Father. He walked in this grace and truth, not looking to the left or to the right. He set His face like a flint; His only purpose was to fulfill His destiny. (Isa. 50:7–10)

Jesus faced betrayal with Judas, one of Jesus' disciples. He taught Judas, He ate with Judas, He relaxed with Judas and, I am sure, He shared His deepest thoughts with Judas. Interestingly, Judas was part of the plan and Jesus chose Him to be a part of His team. Jesus knew what was in Judas' life that would be the open door for the devil to enter. Sometimes the trials we face in life, although not sent by God, are used by God to make us better. Hard times can either make us bitter or better. Judas went down in Bible history as the 'betrayer'.

> My enemies speak evil of me: "When will he die, and his name perish?" And if he comes to see me, he speaks lies; His heart gathers iniquity to itself; When he goes out, he tells it. All who hate me whisper together against me; Against me they devise my hurt. "An evil disease," they say, "clings to him. And now that he lies down, he will rise up no more." Even my own familiar friend in whom I trusted, Who ate my bread, Has lifted up his heel against me. (Ps. 41:5–9)

God wants us to pray for the 'Judas' in our own lives. We must forgive others if we want God to forgive us. (Luke 11:4) I am talking about true forgiveness from the heart, the letting go of the act or acts committed against you. Some of it was willful; some of these acts were demonically inspired. At times it is a combination of both. It doesn't matter; let it go. The devil wants to get you in a position where you are ineffective because of these hurts. Don't allow a root of bitterness to grow in your heart. Your prayers will not avail if you are vengeful, resentful or embittered. You may know all the rules of prayer; you may know all the right ways to pray, but an unforgiving heart aborts your prayers. You are a defiled intercessor.

> Pursue peace with all people, and holiness, without which no one will see the Lord: looking carefully lest anyone fall short of the grace of God; lest any root of bitterness springing up cause trouble, and by this many become defiled. (Heb. 12:14, 15)

We desire revival? Well, my friend, revival begins in us. You can pray all the revival scriptures that are contained in the Word of God. Revival will not happen until true heart forgiveness flows from the church. Instead of accusing our accusers, we must pray for them, thus resulting in help for them and a clean heart for us.

Jesus said, "Father, forgive them, for they do not know what they do." (Luke 23:34) Here, just before Jesus died, He intercedes for His enemies. He lays one hand on His accusers and one hand on His Father. He asks for mercy on their behalf. His accusers were so deceived that they actually thought they were doing God a service by nailing Jesus to the cross. (John 16:2) Deception had their minds blinded.

They may be believers or nonbelievers. If they are believers and they have not stopped their destructive behavior, they are on a road to what the Bible calls a possible shipwreck. They think they are right, but they are deceived. They are blasphemers, not teachable and hardhearted. (2 Tim. 3:2) The pride of their heart will not allow them to let go of their demonically–inspired thought or prejudices. Don't allow their words or actions to hinder your faith; forgive them. Unless there is repentance on their part, they will self–destruct. There is a dual working of the unseen realm; the attitude of a person's heart and the demon activity that is allowed to enter because of this unrepented sin. Pharaoh's pride eventually destroyed him and his army. Judas' love of money entrapped him. Satan had an open door to enter him, thus leading him down a road of eventual suicide. (John 13:2; Matt. 27:5) Fortunately, when he saw that he had betrayed 'innocent blood,' Judas regretted what he did, but it was too late. He couldn't live with himself; I am sure guilt consumed him. We know God would have restored him. Peter is another example of betrayal. Peter too was one of Jesus' disciples. Peter denied Jesus; his betrayal was born out of fear.

> And the Lord said, "Simon, Simon! Indeed, Satan has asked for you, that he may sift you as wheat. But I have prayed for you, that your faith should not fail; and when you have returned to Me, strengthen your brethren." But he said to Him, "Lord, I am ready to go with You, both to prison and to death. Then He said, "I tell you, Peter, the

rooster shall not crow this day before you will deny three times that you know Me." (Luke 22:31–34)

Jesus saw ahead of time that Peter was going to deny Him. The deception was that he thought he would not get caught. God sees and hears everything. There is no running away from His presence. The knowledge of Peter's denial of Him did not take Jesus by surprise, nor did it offend Him. Instead, He was moved with compassion and prayed for Peter. He prayed ahead of time that 'his faith fail not'. Love covers a multitude of sin. The love of God flowing through you in prayer will cover them and protect them, for love never fails. Remember this simple truth: people who hurt people are angry and hurting inside. Maybe at some period in their life some terrible tragedy happened to them. Insecure people gossip, lash out and devour others with their words. When you intercede for this person or persons, you will begin to see them as God sees them. At first it may be difficult for you to pray for this person. Start out by faith, not by what you are feeling. As you walk in a consistent lifestyle of prayer, you will be changed. You will become more and more like the one you are spending time with, God, who is love. He takes no account to the evil done to it, pays no attention to a suffered wrong. Walking in love is walking in the spirit. You will be able to discern you have tapped into a new level when you automatically enter into intercession with no thought of self, no thought about what they said or did. Flesh (human emotion) will not interfere with the will of God. God's will for that person is that they would be saved and come to the knowledge of the truth. You are the laborer that has been sent into their life to pray for them. Just do it, and great will be your reward. You are seeking only to please the Father. You are setting your attention on things above, not on the things of this earth. This life is but a vapor; it appears for a while and then vanishes away. Your obedience to God while on this earth will affect your position in heaven. This life on earth is temporal; the life to come is eternal. It doesn't matter what they did, just pray for them.

> Repay no one evil for evil. Have regard for good things in the sight of all men. If it is possible, as much as depends on you, live peaceably with all men. Beloved, do not avenge yourselves, but rather give place to wrath; for it is

written, "Vengeance is Mine, I will repay," says the Lord. Therefore "If your enemy is hungry, feed him; If he is thirsty, give him a drink; For in so doing you will heap coals of fire on his head." Do not be overcome by evil, but overcome evil with good. (Rom. 12:17–21)

Intercession overcomes the evil with what is good. They need mercy extended on their behalf. Pray for them that mercy would be extended to them. Pray that their eyes would be open to the truth of God's unconditional love for them. An understanding of this truth will set them free. Don't allow the sun to go down on your wrath. Sin not with anger towards them; allow the love of God to dominate your desire to vindicate yourself. Let God arise in your life and your enemies will scatter. (Ps. 68:1) Your prayers are a delight to the Lord; they please Him. When a man's ways please the Lord, He will make his enemies to be at peace with him. (Prov.15:8; 16:7)

Our prayers are eternal; the prayer for Peter was made ahead of time on his behalf. There may be times you have a sense of an impending danger, or something coming that is unfavorable on behalf of a person. At times, intercessors who are trained and sensitive to the Holy Spirit may sense an entrapment coming.

Jesus knew by the 'word of wisdom' that Satan was going to take advantage of Peter's weakness and seek to entrap him. (1 Cor. 12:8–11) Jesus prayed for him and then gave him instruction to go and "strengthen your brethren". Jesus' prayers availed much. So do yours. Peter overcame his weakness; he was strengthened and thus fulfilled his destiny.

As you stand in the gap, the Holy Spirit is stirring within them. You are also 'bearing up, with the idea of completely removing the deception from their eyes'. Now it is their choice. Intercession will not override a person's will. We all have the freedom of choice. You cannot make a person change; you can only prepare the way, till the ground of their heart, use the authority through the name of Jesus on their behalf, and the rest is up to that individual. You were obedient to the call to prayer; the rest is up to them.

Prayer for the Ministry Gifts

Chapter 15

When He ascended on high, He led captivity captive, and gave gifts to men ... And He Himself gave some to be apostles, some prophets, some evangelists, and some pastors and teachers, for the equipping of the saints for the work of ministry, for the edifying of the body of Christ, till we all come to the unity of the faith and of the knowledge of the Son of God, to a perfect man, to the measure of the stature of the fullness of Christ; that we should no longer be children, tossed to and fro and carried about with every wind of doctrine, by the trickery of men, in the cunning craftiness of deceitful plotting, but, speaking the truth in love, may grow up in all things into Him who is the head—Christ—from whom the whole body, joined and knit together by what every joint supplies, according to the effective working by which every part does its share, causes growth of the body for the edifying of itself in love. (Eph. 4:8, 11–16)

When Jesus ascended to His Father, the Bible says, "He led captivity captive and gave gifts unto men." These gifts are called ministry gifts. The primary purpose of these gifts is to perfect, or mature, the body of Christ. The word "perfect" in the Greek translation is *kartartismos* and means "to completely furnish" or "to thoroughly equip". The Lord achieves His purpose through these five ministry gifts. First, God desires that we all come to the unity of the faith. In order for the body of Christ to be in unity, there must be the right teaching, all centered on the transcending principles of Jesus Christ rather than a man-made doctrine. Secondly, the ministry gifts are called to teach the 'milk' of the Word so that believers can grow and mature. (1 Pet. 2:2) Thirdly, the ministry gifts are to train the church in how to operate in their personal, individual callings and, ultimately, each member finding and fulfilling his or her destiny. To grow in our destiny, we are not growing up into a job but into a person––Jesus Christ. All true New Testament ministries are found in Him. Finally, it is important that churches build one another up and improve one another.

Each gift has a different function. There is a different anointing that goes with each of these ministry gifts. These gifts are laid out here in this scripture. They are apostles, prophets, evangelists, pastors and teachers.

These ministry gifts are sovereignly given, and receive their call from God before the person is even formed in their mother's womb. (Jer. 1:5) The ministry gifts that are within men and women today have been raised up by God to live in such a time as this. They are called to speak to this generation. They have a mandate from God to fulfill. One day they will stand before God and give an account for what they did with what they were given.

These five fold ministry gifts have a divine destiny both to be discovered and to be accomplished. Now every believer in the New Testament church is called to witness for Jesus as said in the great commission. There is a destiny for all believers to fulfill. (Mark 16:15–18) But these Christ–given gifts of ministry are purpose–driven. They are called to take the leadership in the church, and to be role models to the believers. They have a responsibility to watch over the souls that are in their care. They have a specific function to carry out. They have a result to achieve. Their personal preparation through prayer, study of the Scriptures, humility and faithfulness to God all contribute in the timing for the gift that is within them to be unwrapped. (1 Tim. 1:12; 2 Tim. 2:15) The prayers of faithful intercessors can also help contribute to the success of a ministry or a church. Ultimately, a man's gift will make room for itself. God is the One to bring them before great men, but don't think that the devil won't try to stop this from happening. (Prov. 18:16)

The ministry gifts need prayer support that will aid them in fulfilling their call. Intercession for the ministry gifts is a supportive ministry. They need our support in prayer. It is done in the secret place before God and not to be seen by men. No hoopla, no fanfare, no flags, no bragging that you possibly were the reason they were so anointed.

As you stand before God in intercession on behalf of the ministry gifts, remember it is not to be done with the wrong motive, meaning that you pray your own will on them or pray what you think they ought to do or say. When praying for pastors and leaders, you are to pray the Word of God over them and not the word of gossip that you overheard from another person in the church or ministry team. God does not hear the prayers of a critical heart. A true intercessor believes the best of their leader, and will not be jealous or resentful toward the man or woman of God. A true intercessor for a ministry gift will have absolute unconditional love for the man or woman of God and desire only to see God's will accomplished in their life and ministry. As you pray for your pastor or any church leader, it is the greatest act of love you can do for them. As you operate in this kind of love, you are releasing the ministry of Jesus on their behalf.

> Now Amalek came and fought with Israel in Rephidim. And Moses said to Joshua, "Choose us some men and go out, fight with Amalek. Tomorrow I will stand on the top of the hill with the rod of God in my hand." So Joshua did as Moses said to him, and fought with Amalek. And Moses, Aaron, and Hur went up to the top of the hill. And so it was, when Moses held up his hand, that Israel prevailed; and when he let down his hand, Amalek prevailed. But Moses' hands became heavy; so they took a stone and put it under him, and he sat on it. And Aaron and Hur supported his hands, one on one side, and the other on the other side; and his hands were steady until the going down of the sun. So Joshua defeated Amalek and his people with the edge of the sword. (Exod. 17:8–13)

A true intercessor for these leaders will hold up the arms of the ministry gift and support the work of God through him or her. Moses is the man of God. He has the rod of God in his hand. He is the leader. Every time the New Testament church succeeds or fails it is primarily because of leadership. Here we see in this verse Moses had become weary, so he needed support. Two men with the right motive came alongside to support him so that the work of God and the will of God could be accomplished.

As we lay down our lives in intercession for these ministry gifts, we are really interceding for the ministry of Jesus to be revealed in the earth. It is and always will be about Him—not a man, a denomination, or human personality. These leaders are called to fully preach the Word. They are ministers that were made according to the gift of the grace of God. This grace given enables them to preach and to operate in their calling. (Eph. 3:1–10) The apostle said, "I am what I am by the grace of God."

I was speaking on the subject of prayer in a church on the East Coast. When I got up to minister, I sensed opposition in the unseen realm. As I began to minister, because of the anointing and the power of the Word, I was able to press through. As time went by it became more difficult for me to effectively minister my message. I then began to feel as though my words were hitting the ceiling and were not having an effect on those in attendance. In the secret place of my heart, I questioned God. He told me not to be concerned; He would take care of it. As I continued to teach, I was aware of a shield of light being formed around me from front to back. I was protected in this bubble of light and love. The ministry of the Word was then released in greater power and freedom as a result of this divine protection.

When I finished my message, I told the congregation to stand. As they stood up, I was drawn to a young man in the back of the church. With all boldness and confidence, I pointed to him and said, "Young man, you need to fear God." I did not know who he was. As a matter of fact, I was so compelled by the Holy Spirit within me, it was as if I were watching myself point him out and speak those words to him. I then found myself saying, "I command the fear of God to come upon you in the name of Jesus." That command of faith surprised me as well as others in the church that was not aware of the unseen conflict going on in the service. With that being said, the young man grabbed his girlfriend and literally ran out of that church. As some of the members in the church were rejoicing, I continued to say, "No man will mock my God". At the conclusion of that service, three ladies came up to me and told me that as I began to minister the Word of God, this man pulled out tarot cards and was attempting to control the flow of God's Spirit in me. They told me he was a known warlock in their city. The devil had sent him to our meeting because I am sure he knew I would be teaching those believers how to pray. He knew the power of prayer and wanted to stop me from bringing forth that message. My assignment was to teach them how to pray; the devil's assignment was to hinder this message from going forth. The devil knew what would happen if these believers tapped into the power of prayer. This message would set others free and that region would not perish because of a lack of knowledge concerning prayer and spiritual warfare. (Hosea 4:6; John 8:32)

If the devil can stop the minister, he can stop the people from moving forward into their destinies. These intercessors saw what this young man was attempting to do through evil powers, and instead of just sitting there and 'taking it,' they decided to 'take their place' in prayer. They quietly took authority over the works of darkness and any demonic influence in that service through the name of Jesus. (Mark 16:17; Luke 10:17–20) When God told me not to be concerned; He would take care of it (the warfare), He knew He was going to find faithful intercessors who would stand in the gap and pray for the ministry gift who was sent by God to minister the Word to them. They did their part, and we had a successful service.

About a year later, we returned to that same church where this had taken place. The same young man came up to me and asked me if I remembered him. I did not. He told me he was involved in witchcraft, and reminded me of that particular night. He told me that since the meeting, he had accepted Jesus into his heart and had been born again! What a testimony of God's power, His grace and His love!

> Finally, brethren, pray for us, that the word of the Lord may run swiftly and be glorified, just as it is with you, and that we may be delivered from unreasonable and wicked men; for not all have faith. (2 Thess. 3:1–2)

Paul is asking for prayer. He is specific about his request. His request is that the word of the Lord may have free course. He desired that what was within him would flow forth with ease and with revelation. A minister spends time with God through prayer and through study in the Scriptures. He has the gifting to operate in his calling. He has prepared, and now he has direction as to what needs to be ministered to the people who will be gathered together to hear the Word of the Lord. Paul's desire is that what has been planted in his heart will have free course. His desire is that what is in abundance in his heart will have free course, be gladly received, planted and ultimately bear fruit. (Matt. 12:24) Paul is anticipating warfare in the spirit, and therefore is asking for support from other believers.

Warfare can manifest in the spirit realm from different sources. It may come from strongholds that are keeping a city or congregation bound, or from the attitudes of the people in attendance. Satan is the god of this world, and when Holy Spirit filled ministers come into their town, they will try to stop the move of God with warfare. This warfare can come from the spirits that rule over those areas that have not yet been dethroned. The warfare a minister may encounter from the people is the attitudes of the heart that are unseen. These attitudes will affect the flow of the Word of God and the flow of the Holy Spirit. Paul's prayer request is that he would have favor with the people, and that the teaching of the Word would bear fruit (Mark 4:14–20); prayer that what was in his heart would flow easily and quickly to the people to whom God had sent him to minister; prayer that the ministry of Jesus would manifest through his earthen vessel. This same request goes forth from the hearts of the leadership today.

> For a wide door of opportunity for effectual (service) has opened to me (there, a great and promising one), and (there are) many adversaries. (1 Cor. 16:9) (AMP)

> Continue earnestly in prayer, being vigilant in it with thanksgiving, meanwhile praying also for us, that God would open to us a door for the word, to speak the mystery of Christ, for which I am also in chains, that I may make it manifest, as I ought to speak. (Col. 4:2–4)

Here, Paul is again asking for prayer. He is not too proud to ask! He knew he needed the prayer support of faithful intercessors. He again is asking for freedom of speech, but he is also asking for doors to be open on his behalf, so that the message he has been entrusted with goes forth! Intercession opens up doors and makes a way for the Gospel. We have not, because we ask not. Man is God's avenue into the earth. Pray for doors to open up in behalf of the ministry gifts!

> And for me, that utterance may be given to me, that I may open my mouth boldly, to make known the mystery of the gospel, for which I am an ambassador in bonds; that therein I may speak boldly, as I ought to speak. (Eph. 6:18–20)

Paul should have always been able to speak boldly, but at times, just like our leaders today, there are hindrances! Command the hindrances to be removed in the name of Jesus! Prayer will remove those hindrances and cause boldness to rise up in the ministry gifts.

I must continue to emphasize how important it is that you pray the Word of God over these ministers and not your own will as it relates to decisions that they make concerning the work God has called them to oversee. Praying the Word and praying in the spirit is always the correct method of intercession. Your will is nowhere to be found, just your obedience to pray and to love them unconditionally. Most pastors and ministers want to do the right thing before God. At times they might need direction or clarification, or maybe they are deceived into believing a lie instead of the truth. Intercession can help to remove these obstacles so that the light of God can shine on their ways. Intercession helps them to be able to see clearly with the eyes of their spirit.

> Always laboring fervently for you in prayers, that you may stand perfect and complete in all the will of God. (Col. 4:12)

> I do not cease to pray for you, and to ask that you may be filled with the knowledge of His will in all wisdom and spiritual understanding; that you may walk worthy of the Lord, fully pleasing Him, and being fruitful in every good work and increasing in the knowledge of God;

strengthened with all might, according to His glorious power. (Col. 1:9–11)

As a traveling minister, I have always been a trusted friend to many pastors and their wives. I have a reputation for being a "keeper of the secrets" of these men and women who are at times in need of prayer and counsel. If you are a minister involved in prayer or counseling and can't keep their secrets, you are not only touching the anointed of God, but you are tearing down the very kingdom you profess to be building up. God will not only hold you accountable, but how can He tell you the deeper secrets of His heart and bring you to the next level? You are not walking in love, and you are sowing discord among your fellow ministers. This is one of the things God hates. (Prov. 6:16–19) Your prayers will be hindered and ultimately so will your ministry. God knows whom He can trust when it comes to prayer assignments that relate to His ministers.

I have certain minister friends I am 'on call' for as the Spirit wills. The manifestation of these prayer assignments comes in various ways, depending on the mind of the Holy Spirit and how He wills to bring it to me. There is one particular minister friend I have known for over thirty years. I have a great love and respect for this minister. I don't need to talk with this individual often, but I am there as an unspoken support. There have been a few times when I do let this individual know what God has had me to pray, but I am very cautious in this regard because I do not want to grieve the Holy Spirit, and therefore have His anointing lift. Praying for His ministers is a holy thing. God is very protective of His ministers.

My prayer assignments for this individual used to come mostly through 'having this person on my heart' or a 'tangible love in my inner man' that was as real as a pregnancy. This burden had form and move-ment, so to speak. Over the past four years, the delivery of these prayer assignments for this individual has changed. Now, they come suddenly and in the night through a 'God dream'. The dream is visionary in a sense and carries with it much detail of what is or what is to come or both. In these prayer assignments, I am given the exact scriptures with which to pray. After praying these scriptures, I give myself over to the Holy Spirit. I pray in tongues all the while knowing in part (according to the scrip-tures given) what is in the mind of God. The last assignment I had for this minister lasted three days. It was a prayer burden that was with me when I got up in the morning and when I laid down at night. I even spent an hour or so before going to sleep, praying the Scriptures and praying in tongues until I fell off to sleep, only to have the Lord wake me up in the middle of the night to continue. I believe God has given me more prophetic insight into this person's life because He knows I will keep it a private matter. On occasion, I pray as to whether or not to share the scriptures God has given me. When I do share them, I do so with much fear and trembling, with the knowledge that I am speaking to God's anointed.

> But Peter, standing up with the eleven, raised his voice and said to them. (Acts 2:14)

The Holy Spirit had just been poured out. The visitation of the Spirit had finally come. Revelation knowledge had just been released. Peter is another ministry gift spoken of in the Word of God. Let's take a look at the effect his ministry had on the church in his day. Of the eleven that were with Peter, he was the vessel God chose at that moment to preach. He stands up, lifts up his voice, and he has freedom of speech. He is operating in his calling, he is anointed with fresh oil, and he is bold to speak the Word. He begins to preach from the book of Joel about the last days and how God is going to pour out His Spirit. Those who gladly received his word were baptized; and that day about three thousand souls were added to them. (Acts 2:37–41) Peter is an example of one man operating in his calling with freedom! Three thousand souls were born into the Kingdom of God in one day! Glory to God!

There are ministries God is raising up for these last days. The things God desires to release will astound many. He is in the process of raising mouthpieces in the land who will speak for Him and not hold back. He is raising ministries who will carry the torch of revival to other lands. They need our prayer support.

What you do in secret on behalf of these ministers and leaders will be rewarded to you when you stand before God. In this place of prayer, you have entered into their labors. They have a public ministry, and yours is in private. As you pray for these leaders and ministries, do not expect to receive any acclamation from any person on this earth. Again, remember your reward will come from your Father in heaven.

In Acts chapter 3, Peter and John went up together to the temple for prayer. As they began to enter into the temple, they saw a certain man lame from his mother's womb. This man would lie there at the gate and beg for money from anyone who passed by. When Peter and John were about to go into the temple, they were drawn to this man. Peter fixed his eyes upon him. He said, "Silver and gold I do not have, but what I do have I give you, in the name of Jesus Christ of Nazareth, rise up and walk." This man was instantly healed! Now you would think that everyone would have been happy about this miracle that had occurred. Well, they were not! Some men were angry and jealous about what had just happened! In the 4th chapter of Acts, we find that the religious leaders of that day were greatly disturbed that they taught the people and preached about Jesus and the resurrection from the dead. By now, as a result of this miracle and preaching, five thousand souls had been saved! They decided to take Peter and John into custody. The disciples were severely threatened by these religious leaders. They are told not to preach nor teach at all in the name of Jesus. These threats did not shake these ministers. They know the power of unity and the power of prayer.

> And being let go, they went to their own companions and reported all that the chief priests and elders had said to them. So when they heard that, they raised their voice to God with one accord and said; "Lord, You are God, who made heaven and earth and the sea, and all that is in them. Now, Lord, look on their threats, and grant to Your servants that with all boldness they may speak Your word, by stretching forth Your hand to heal, and that signs and wonders may be done through the name of Your holy Servant Jesus." And when they had prayed, the place where they were assembled together was shaken; and they were all filled with the Holy Spirit, and they spoke the word of God with boldness. (Acts 4:23–24; 29–31)

They prayed for boldness in the midst of warfare. They acknowledged God's provision in His protection of them. They even prayed for more miracles to manifest. As a result of their prayers, great grace continued to be upon them. Miracles followed the preaching of the Word, so much so that Peter's shadow brought healing to the sick. (Acts 5:12, 15) Your prayers on behalf of the ministry gifts will produce the same results as you pray these scriptures for them!

Peter was therefore kept in prison, but constant prayer was offered to God for him by the church. And when Herod was about to bring him out, that night Peter was sleeping, bound with two chains between two soldiers; and the guards before the door were keeping the prison. Now behold, an angel of the Lord stood by him, and a light shone in the prison; and he struck Peter on the side and raised him up, saying, "Arise quickly!" And his chains fell off his hands. Then the angel said to him, "Gird yourself and tie on your sandals;" and so he did. And he said to him, "Put on your garment and follow me." So he went out and followed him, and he did not know that what was done by the angel was real, but thought he was seeing a vision. When they were past the first and second guard posts, they came to the iron gate that leads to the city, which opened to them of its own accord; and they went out and went down one street, and immediately the angel departed from him. And when Peter had come to himself, he said, "Now I know for certain that the Lord has sent His angel, and has delivered me from the hand of Herod and from all the expectation of the Jewish people." So, when he had considered this, he came to the house of Mary, the mother of John whose surname was Mark, where many were gathered together praying. And as Peter knocked at the door of the gate, a girl named Rhoda came to answer. When she recognized Peter's voice, because of her gladness she did not open the gate, but ran in and announced that Peter stood before the gate. But they said to her, "You are beside yourself!" Yet she kept insisting that it was so. So they said, "It is his angel." Now Peter continued knocking; and when they opened the door and saw him, they were astonished. (Acts 12:5–16)

Peter is the ministry gift. He is a key man in a key position, and he has an assignment. He has been raised up for such a time as this. Where is he? He is in prison. The Word of God is not having free course. During his imprisonment, the church is praying. They are gathered together in corporate intercession on behalf of Peter. In the spirit, they lay one hand on Peter and one hand on God. Notice that Peter is sleeping. Who was doing all the work? The church! They are taking their place in prayer, using their God–given authority, and believing God for a miracle. They decided they were not going to allow Peter to be imprisoned. They knew his ministry had not finished its course and he had the gifting that was needed to fulfill the purposes of God for their generation. They decided to stir themselves up, take hold of God and pray for Peter's deliverance. It was the responsibility of the church to act on his behalf.

The church had a prayer assignment for Peter. God did not raise Peter up for him to be ineffective and in prison. That ministry gift was needed in the earth. The early church needed to hear what God had to say through Peter!

Prayer was made without ceasing unto God for Peter. They were absent from him in the flesh, but they were present with him in the spirit. They don't stop until they see visible results! They are not quitters! God has raised these intercessors up! They know what their purpose is, and they will fulfill their destiny. Peter is not the only key to this move of God; the intercessors who know their God will be strong and do mighty exploits in the secret place. They were coming against the hindrances; they were coming against the circumstances that had him bound. They were asking for supernatural intervention.

As a result of their intercessions, notice angelic activity is released. Pray Psalm 91 over these ministers, especially those who travel for the sake of the Gospel. Just take that particular Psalm, insert their name in it, and pray it out loud before the throne of God. As you pray this Word of God over these leaders, these ministering angels become actively involved. (Ps. 103:20; Heb. 1:14) Your prayers will keep a hedge of protection around them.

Before Peter's release comes, a light shines in the prison. As you intercede for the ministry gifts, pray Ephesians 1:15–23 for them. Insert their name in these verses. Pray that as they study their Bible, the "entrance of His Word would bring light". (Ps. 119:130) Your prayers will ultimately affect you, because if he or she is your pastor, you will hear the fresh revelation that they bring forth from the pulpit. (1 Cor. 4:16)

Notice that Peter is raised up. As you stand with them in intercession, they will continue to be raised up to the place God has called them. The angel then says again, "Rise up quickly!" Run with the vision! As leaders spend time in the presence of God, He writes the vision, the plan for their church or ministry, on their hearts. As these leaders set their hearts to obey God fully, they may also need to let go of any weights or 'chains' that keep them from advancing forward in their calling. (Heb. 12:1–2) Your prayers will support these leaders as they run with the vision God has given them. Intercession for the ministry gifts will assist in the letting go of anything that has not been born of God.

As prayer is being made without ceasing for Peter, the angel tells him to "Gird yourself and tie on your sandals ... put on your garment and follow me". To "gird" as defined in Webster's dictionary, is "to prepare oneself for action". Maybe you know of a minister who has laid down their ministry because of discouragement or sin. The callings of God are without repentance. (Rom. 11:29) When God calls a man or a woman, they may live and die without fulfilling that call, but this does not change God's mind about His choice for picking them for service.

The callings of God are irrevocable. Pray that they would be restored. The Spirit of the Lord is upon them and God has anointed them to preach the Gospel. Their feet are shod with the Gospel of peace, deliverance and healing. They need to "tie on those sandals" once again. Woe to these leaders, if they do not fulfill their destiny. (1 Cor. 9:16) They are unhappy and unfulfilled. They are like Jonah, disobedient to the heavenly vision and running from God. They may be sitting in a church, but there is a gaping hole of unfulfillment within their soul. Release compassion and intercede for these precious fallen soldiers. God not only wants them restores, He desires that the glory of their latter end would be greater than their former. They need encouragement and prayer. God desires to anoint our leaders with fresh oil.

The angel tells Peter to "put on your garment and follow me". To me, metaphorically, the garment speaks of the spiritual gifting, anointing and spiritual authority that the five fold ministry gifts are called to walk in. Biblically, the leaders under the Old Testament dressed for their office, and they were identified by what they wore. For example, kings and queens dressed for their position. Under the Levitical Law, the priests had to wear designated clothing, and even the military were distinguished by what they wore. Think about Elisha. He picked up the mantle that fell from Elijah. He put it on– there was power in that mantle! The mantle or garments represented their authority and even gave them their identity. The angel told Peter to put it back on. The Lord Jesus has called these ministry gifts and He desires that they walk in the fullness of their anointing. If they have laid their garment down, the Lord desires that they put back on the garment of anointing that they once walked in.

Prayer continues to be made without ceasing for Peter. The intercessors are unaware that Peter is being released; they are walking by faith and not by sight. They know God answers prayer and they are still not released from praying for him. They are on assignment! The angel takes Peter past the first and second guard posts. This speaks to me regarding phases, times and seasons of every life and ministry. Prayer prepares the way for the next phase of ministry for a minister. Peter passes through the first "phase", then the second "phase", and now he comes to a door, or an iron gate that leads into the city. His steps are being ordered and established by God. (Ps. 37:23) Their prayers are producing divine direction. Peter is moving toward his destiny.

> And to the angel of the church in Philadelphia write, These things say He who is holy, He who is true, He who has the key of David, He who opens and no one shuts, and shuts and no one opens. I know your works. See, I have set before you an open door, and no one can shut it. (Revelation 3:7, 8)

There are ministers who are called to a city. There are ministers who are called to a nation. There are ministers who are called to the world. Wherever they are called, they are anointed; God has commissioned them for that particular place, and therefore He has given them that land. Now they must possess it. (Josh. 1:3) Remember what Paul said in 1 Corinthians 16:9? He said that a door of opportunity had been opened to him, but there were many hindrances. Through intercession, hindrances are removed so that the gate or the door opens, bringing our leaders into the possession of their territories. Not by might, not by human strength, but by the Spirit of the Lord, through the preaching of the Word of God and faithful, supportive intercessors. In the event that the minister you are praying for is a traveling minister, pray that God would give him favor, and therefore open doors or opportunities for his or her ministry.

God gives the ministry gifts, the call and the vision. We the church aid and assist these leaders in breaking through. I have seen churches have a special groundbreaking service as they enter into a new building project but I often wonder how many of these churches have broken ground in the spirit. That area is ours legally, but vitally we must take it.

Peter was at the gate that led into the city. When he got to the door, it opened to him on its own accord. He didn't even have to lift a finger. The prayers of the church had already done the work for him. It is not up to the minister to do all the work, so don't expect him to. We are a body, fitly joined together by that which every joint supplies, and Christ is the head of His church. (Eph. 4:16) We will see the fulfillment of God's heart complete in the earth; but it is going to take all of us to get the job accomplished.

The angel departs from Peter. He has been delivered from the hand of Herod and from all the expectations of the Jewish people. He goes to the house of Mary where many were gathering for prayer. He knocks at the door of the house, Rhoda goes to the door to answer, recognizes Peter's voice, and that is him who is standing outside. Instead of opening the door and letting him in, she goes back and tells the others that Peter is outside. They thought she was beside herself; in other words, that she was crazy! They then go on to say that it must be his angel. Peter just continued knocking, and when they had opened the door and saw him, they were astonished! Don't be astonished when you see that your prayers have been answered.

United Prayer

Chapter 16

My house shall be called a house of prayer for all nations.
(Isa. 56:7)

*I*ndividually, we are the houses of prayer. Collectively, we too are the houses of prayer. We need to gather together not only to hear the teachings of the Bible but also to join in cooperate united prayer. This type of prayer was a common practice of the early church. The early church was in revival; they saw great moves of God's Spirit. They ministered in such power that everywhere they went the manifested presence of Jesus was apparent. They witnessed miracles after the preaching of the Word of God. The Apostles certainly were not shy; they were bold to speak the Word.

The early church also exercised unity in purpose. It says in 1 Corinthians 1:10, "that you all speak the same thing and that there be no divisions among you; but that you be perfectly joined together in the same mind and in the same judgment." It also says in Psalms 133 that when the brethren are in unity, it is pleasant to God and the blessings of God are released. There is power in unity—unity of purpose and unity in prayer. We know we are not to forsake the assembly of ourselves together for the teaching of the Word of God. Let's take this scripture and put it into the context of corporate intercession. One will chase a thousand to flight; two will put ten thousand to flight. Imagine the power our churches would ignite if there were regular united prayer meetings? Let's look at this type of prayer as it was practiced in the early church.

It says in Acts 1:4–5 that the early church assembled together, waiting for the promise of the baptism of the Holy Spirit. In verse 14 of that same chapter, these all "continued with one accord in prayer and supplication". The disciples had a promise from Jesus. They also had expectation and faith that Jesus would fulfill His promise. More of the plans and purposes of God were about to be born. Their part was to wait and pray. This was a new beginning; this was holy. This was an amazing time in church history. These men and women had to be so tuned in to what was about to happen.

> When the day of Pentecost had fully come they were all with one accord on one place. And suddenly there came a sound from heaven, as of a rushing mighty wind, and it filled the whole house where they were sitting. Then there appeared to them divided tongues, as of fire, and one sat upon each one of them. And they were all filled with the Holy Spirit and began to speak with other tongues, as the Spirit gave them utterance. (Acts 2:1–4)

When the season for rain came, the Holy Spirit was poured out. It was the time and the season for the promise of God to be born in the earth. What God had promised, He was able also to perform. The disciples did what they were commanded to do. God did what He said He would do. The early church was in a time of revival.

Prayer produces intimacy, first with God, then with the people with whom you are praying. Prayer will produce intimacy in your church body. Let us say you have a church where there is a lack of unity and strife exists. The best thing you can do is call your church body for a time of corporate, united prayer. Prayer will change the atmosphere in your church. Prayer will change the attitudes of the people's hearts toward one another. Prayer will unite and people will begin to see each other through the eyes of Jesus. Where there is unity, there is power.

Notice the previous scripture said, "when the fullness of time had come". You could be praying for something for years, months or weeks. When things in the Spirit line up, suddenly things begin to break forth. All things begin to work together for the good. Some of the things we pray for involve timing. When it is the fullness of time, you will see God suddenly show up. Compare it to a woman when she is pregnant. It takes nine long months for the baby to internally grow. The family is excited and the mother is in a state of anticipation. She is getting things ready for the life that is about to be born. She doesn't grow weary or lose heart just because she doesn't see that child outwardly in her arms. She knows it is in the baby's best interest to stay hidden in the womb. She knows that life is being properly nourished and is growing on the inside of her. When the fullness of time comes, the baby is ready and mature. What is in the womb will be born; everyone will see it and rejoice.

The church is pregnant with a promise. This is an exciting time in church history. Those believers who have chosen to pick up the mantle of the ministry of intercessory are a part of the body that is praying for this promise to be born. What is the promise? "For I will pour water upon him that is thirsty, and floods upon the dry ground." (Isa. 44:3) "Ask ye of the Lord rain in the time of the latter rain; so the Lord shall give them showers of rain." (Zech. 10:1) We are not going to faint if we don't see visible results. We are pregnant with a promise and we know that in due season we will reap the manifested presence of God in the earth. With this manifested presence we will reap a harvest of souls because they will see the goodness of God. This manifested presence releases the ministry of the Holy Spirit. His ministry is to "convict and convince the world of their need for Jesus". (John 16:7–11)

Today, God is stirring within believers a burden of prayer. God is calling whole congregations. His call is not just for the individual intercessor in the prayer closet. His call is to all churches across America. He desires to work a work in our land that if we fully realized it, it would seem like a dream. (Hab. 1:5) There has never been so much Bible teaching as well as access through multimedia. The teaching is strong and carries much revelation in God's Word. Let us take this knowledge, this faith, and this agreement into corporate prayer. Churches in America must call solemn assemblies and pray instead of using all of our corporate gatherings to hear Bible teaching. (Joel 1:10–14)

Revival birthed in prayer must also be sustained in prayer. Again, we have the early church as our example. In Acts 4, a cripple man is healed, and the Scribes and Pharisees became angry. Not only was this man healed in the name of Jesus, but also 5,000 souls were added to the church. Now that is revival! These men wanted to stop the move of God. They were angry with Peter and John and wanted them to be stopped. These Scribes and Pharisees were commanded to not teach or preach any longer in the name of Jesus. Look at how the disciples responded:

> And being let go, they went to their own companions and reported all that the chief priests and elders had said to them. So when they heard that, they raised their voice to God with one accord ... And when they had prayed, the place where they were assembled together was shaken, and they were all filled with the Holy Spirit and spoke the word of God with boldness ... great power ... And great grace was upon them all. (Acts 4:23–24, 31, 33)

This was the result of corporate united prayer. They experienced great power, great grace, and miracles. They were in a time of refreshing because of the presence of the Lord. That is what we desire to see. "Oh God, thou art my God; early will I seek thee; my soul thirsteth for thee, my flesh longs for thee in a dry and thirsty land where no water is; to see thy power and thy glory." (Ps. 63:1–2) This is our vision. "Be ye doers of the word, and not hearers only." (James 1:22)

Corporate Tongues:
the Universal Language

Chapter 17

For then I will restore to the peoples a pure language, that they all may call on the name of the Lord, to serve Him with one accord. (Zeph. 3:9)

And these signs will follow those who believe ... they will speak with new tongues. (Mark 16:17)

God is talking about restoring to the earth a pure, universal language. When Jesus fulfilled His promise and sent the Holy Spirit to us, that universal, pure language was given to us. It is the language of the Holy Spirit. When we speak in tongues, we are praying out the perfect plan of God. Corporately, we are stirring up that universal language when we pray in tongues. Even though each individual tongue may sound different to us, corporately, our tongues together are that pure, universal language.

1 Corinthians tells us, "Now I beseech you, brethren, by the name of our Lord Jesus Christ, that ye all speak the same thing and that there be no divisions among you; but that ye be perfectly joined together in the same mind and in the same judgment."

Every individual church, while having its own vision, is a part of the corporate vision of the Holy Spirit. It is important to know the vision of your local church. God gives the vision to the pastor. He in turn imparts that vision to his local flock. Your pastor needs men and women who will join him, not only to do the work of the ministry in the natural (ushering, secretary, worship leader, etc.), but he needs men and women who will take the vision and run with it in intercession. The local congregation must be in agreement with him in faith and in prayer. Work must be done in the spirit as well as in the natural. In the spirit, the way needs to be prepared, and the ground tilled. The plan of God for that area where the church resides must be prayed through and birthed in. The pastor cannot do it alone. He has his part; you have yours.

Let us take a look at an Old Testament example of the power that is available through determination, a universal language, and unity in purpose. This is a negative example, but we will turn it around and show you how this scripture relates to united prayer.

> Now the whole earth had one language and one speech. And it came to pass, as they journeyed from the east, that they found a plain in the land of Shinar, and they dwelt there. Then they said to one another, "Come, let us make bricks and bake them thoroughly." They had brick for stone, and they had asphalt for mortar. And they said, "Come, let us build ourselves a city, and a tower whose top is in the heavens; let us make a name for ourselves, lest we be scattered abroad over the face of the whole earth." But the Lord came down to see the city and the tower which the sons of men had built. And the Lord said, "Indeed the people are one and they all have one language, and this is what they begin to do; now nothing that they propose to do will be withheld from them. Come, let Us go down and there confuse their language, that they may not understand one another's speech." So the Lord scattered them abroad from there over the face of all the earth, and they ceased building the city. (Gen. 11:1–8)

Notice they are all speaking the same thing. They all possessed the same vision. Their desire was to build a tower for their own glory. Notice God's reaction. Because of their unity, God said that nothing that they have imagined to do would be impossible for them. Their unity of speech and unity of vision was so powerful that God had to confound their language and scatter them. If the ungodly have such power because of their unity, what about the church? We desire to see the will of God accomplished in the earth. We desire to build a "city, a tower, and a name" for the King of kings and the Lord of lords. God will bless our plans and our efforts. He has given us His Word, the name of Jesus, and praying in tongues. Let us use our authority, pray the Word of God, and when we know not what else to pray, pray in tongues. Corporately praying in tongues will produce results quicker than if we individually prayed. "One will chase a thousand; two will put ten-thousand to flight."

Watching and Praying—
Soldiers in Prayer

Chapter 18

In conclusion, be strong in the Lord (be empowered through your union with Him); draw your strength from Him (that strength which His boundless might provides) Put on God's whole armor (the armor of a heavy-armed soldier which God supplies), that you may be able to successfully stand up against (all) the strategies and the deceits of the devil. For we wrestle not with flesh and blood (contending only with physical opponents), but against the despotisms, against the powers, against (the master spirit forces who are) the world rulers of this present darkness, against the spirit forces of wickedness in the heavenly (supernatural) sphere. Therefore put on God's complete armor, that you may be able to resist and stand your ground on the evil day (of danger), and, having done all (the crisis demands), to stand (firmly in your place) Stand therefore (hold your ground), having tightened the belt of truth around your loins and having put on the breastplate of integrity and of moral rectitude and right standing with God, and having shod your feet in preparation (to face the enemy with the firm-footed stability, the promptness, and the readiness produced by the good news) of the Gospel of peace. Lift up over all the (covering) shield of saving faith, upon which you can quench all

the flaming missiles of the wicked (one) And take the helmet of salvation and the sword that the Spirit wields, which is the Word of God. Pray at all times (on every occasion, in every season) in the Spirit, with all (manner of) prayer and entreaty. To that end keep alert and watch with strong purpose and perseverance, interceding in behalf of all the saints (God's consecrated people). (Eph. 6:10–18) (AMP)

We have an enemy and we are in a war. You, as an intercessor, are enlisted in God's army as a soldier in prayer. See yourself as you are. You are a soldier, complete with God's full armor. You have everything you need to take the enemy on and win every time. Jesus already defeated the devil, and now as we pray we manifest the finished work of our dominion over darkness.

You are clothed with the full armor of God. This is armor that protects you as you begin to go into battle against the forces of darkness. When you pray the Word of God and use the name of Jesus, the devil does not see you in the flesh. He sees Jesus coming after him. You don't have to be afraid of the devil. "Greater is He that is in you than He that is in the world." God has trained you as His soldier; you are equipped. Now go, therefore, and take the land that is legally yours. You are called to be a soldier to possess ground for the kingdom of God. Up until now, the church has been in boot camp. We have been trained in the Word of God. We have learned the power of praying in tongues. We have been trained to use our faith, and what the force of faith will produce. We understand what salvation means and who we are in Christ. We know we are the righteousness of God in Christ, and that we are complete in Him. Not in our righteousness, but in HIM! This is the armor of God! It's that simple. God never called the church to walk in something without fully equipping us to do these exploits. In these last days, the people who know their God will prove themselves strong and shall stand firm and do exploits for God. (Dan. 11:32) We are called to know our God intimately and do exploits for Him. Not just publicly, but in the secret place of prayer.

Notice the last verse of the above scripture, "Praying always and watching." Watching and praying go hand in hand; you cannot separate the two. For an intercessor to be successful in their prayer assignment, it requires that he or she be watchful. The word for "watching" in Greek is *agrupneo*. This word means, "to be sleepless, not just mere wakefulness, but the watchfulness of those who are intent upon a thing". What are we intent on as it relates to prayer? Results! We desire God's will to be done on earth as it is in heaven. We will not stop. We will not back down. We, as intercessors, will fulfill our destiny. We will obey God! We will run and not grow weary; we will walk out our prayer assignments and we will not faint. Jesus said in Luke 18:1, "Men ought always to pray, and not to faint." People are depending on us. Our cities are depending on us.

Notice that the definition also says that we are not only to be awake, but watchful! What does that mean? It is one thing to be awake, and another thing to be both awake and watchful. For example, let's say your TV is on and you go to the news channel so that you can observe world events. You want to know what is happening across the world as it relates to current events. It is one thing for you to watch and listen to the program, and another thing for you to have the TV on the correct channel and not be paying attention. As soldiers, we must pay attention! Pay attention to the atmosphere in your city, your nation. Pay attention to a possible weapon that the enemy may be forming against a loved one, or a national leader. Be on guard on their behalf. Pay attention! Be alert! We are not to be ignorant of Satan's devises. Pray for discernment. God will give you what you desire as you seek Him first. The gift of discerning of spirits is not just for the minister who speaks in the pulpit. This gift has been given to the church, looking not with your physical eyes, but with the eyes of your spirit. Put up your spiritual antenna, so to speak. Pray for your eyes to be enlightened so that you can be accurate in intercession. Be in tune. Be on guard. Be alert.

Continue in prayer and watch. (Col. 4:2)

The word "watch" in this text is *gregoro*. It means to watch and is used in keeping awake, in spiritual alertness. Be watchful. Be vigilant. Continue in prayer until released by the Holy Spirit; continue and be spiritually alert.

Be ye therefore sober, and watch unto prayer. (1 Pet. 4:7)

Again, the word *gregoro* is used. In this text He is also telling us to be sober. The word "sober" is the Greek word *sophroneo*. This word means "to think soberly, to be sober minded". Webster's defines sober as "not intoxicated or drunk, habitually temperate, marked by seriousness, gravity or tone". Understand the seriousness of the call to prayer. Be sober; be alert. We are truly in a spiritual war. It is with the unseen forces of darkness that desire to keep our cities, our nations and our families in chains. Know who your enemy is and cast him out!

> Accordingly then, let us not sleep, as the rest do, but let us keep wide awake (alert, watchful, cautious, and on our guard) and let us be sober (calm, collected, and circumspect) For those who sleep, sleep in the night, and those who are drunk, get drunk at night. But we belong to the day; therefore, let us be sober and put on the breastplate (corset) of faith and love and for a helmet the hope of salvation. (1 Thess. 5:6–8) (AMP)

In this scripture, again the armor is mention. Love is also mentioned as it relates to our spiritual armor. As we walk in new levels of intercession, it is important that there be no cracks or exposed areas in our armor. What do I mean by that? It means walk in love and forgive. Pray for your enemies and your accusers. If you have any wounds or unforgiveness, that is an open door for the enemy to take advantage of you. This is simple truth. Watch your love walk and stay close to Him.

When Jesus came to the earth as an intercessor, He too had on armor. Let's look at Isaiah 59:16–18:

> He saw that there was no man, and wondered that there was no intercessor; therefore His own arm brought salvation for Him; and His own righteousness, it sustained Him. For He put on righteousness as a breastplate, and a helmet of salvation on His head; He put on the garments of vengeance for clothing, and was clad with zeal as a cloak. (NKJV)

Jesus was clad with zeal as a cloak. Webster's defines zeal as "fervor for a person or an object; eager desire or endeavor; enthusiastic diligence". We have an enemy that goes around seeking whom he may devour. Notice that part of Jesus' armor was to be fervent, diligent, and enthusiastic. Discouragement is the enemy of successful results. Don't give up. Don't faint if you don't see visible results. Hope deferred makes the heart sick. (Prov. 13:12) Faith is the substance of things hoped for, the evidence of things that are not seen. Ground is being taken in the unseen realm. Keep the switch of faith turned on. If you begin to lose hope, you are beginning to let the things you have heard slip. Don't allow yourself to fall into discouragement or depression. As soldiers, we need to keep up the morale. Encourage and strengthen yourself in the Lord, as David did. (1 Sam. 30:6) He too was a mighty soldier and was mighty in battle! Well, how do you do that? Begin to rehearse all the victories in prayer you have seen manifested. Go to the book of Psalms and read them out loud or even sing them. Speak the Word out loud so your ears hear the Scriptures.

Watchmen on the Wall

Chapter 19

Unless the Lord builds the house, they labor in vain who build it; unless the Lord guards the city, the watchman stays awake in vain. (Ps. 127:1)

An intercessor is a watchman. He is the one who does the watching in prayer. Webster's defines watchman as "a person hired to guard or watch, especially at night". The James Moffatt translation of that verse says, "Unless the Eternal builds the house, workmen build in vain; unless the Eternal guards the town, sentries are on guard in vain." The word "sentries" in Webster's is defined, "a person, especially a soldier, stationed to guard as group against surprise".

Who is our enemy? John 10:10 says that the thief come to kill, steal and to destroy. The enemy is no other than the devil. We are enlisted by God to be an intercessor. He has hired us. He had called us. He has equipped us.

The Hebrew word for "watchman" is *shamar*. The definition is "to hedge about as with thorns, to protect, to attend to, to look narrowly, to preserve". Another word is *tsapah*, which is defined as "to lean forward, to peer into the distance, to observe, await, behold, to look up, wait for, keep the watch, watchman".

I have set watchmen upon your walls, O Jerusalem, who will never hold their peace day or night; you who (are

His servants and by your prayers) put the Lord in remembrance (of His promises), keep not silence, and give Him no rest until He establishes Jerusalem and makes her a praise in the earth. (Isa. 62:6, 7) (AMP)

I want you to notice where he is positioned. He is positioned on the walls. Because of his position on the wall, he is able to see trouble coming from afar. He is able to peer into the distance! That, to me, speaks of discernment; knowing of the enemy's whereabouts and plans before he strikes, aborting his plans and purposes, and stopping the attack so that we are not taken by surprise! If our homeland security had heard of the terrorist attacks on September 11, 2001 before they happened, we would not have lost so many lives. We would not be troubled with thoughts of terror and fear.

Prepare the table, set a watchman in the tower ... Go, set a watchman, let him declare what he sees. (Isa. 21: 5, 6)

As intercessors we are in a position to see things before they happen. Our job is to protect the good that is within the city walls. God cares for our cities and nations because they contain people.

But the land which you cross over to possess is a land of hills and valleys, which drinks water from the rain of heaven, a land for which the Lord your God cares; the eyes of the Lord your God are always on it, from the beginning of the year to the very end of the year. (Deut. 11:11–12)

Notice that the watchman brings to God His Word. We bring to Him what He said. We are not trying to talk Him into something; He already desires to fulfill His will on earth. Prayer is not talking God into something. Man is God's legal avenue into this earth. We are releasing His plans and purposes for our land as we release the Scriptures from our mouth to His ears.

For I know the thoughts I think toward you, says the Lord, thoughts of peace and not of evil, to give you a future and a hope. (Jer. 29:11)

And the Lord appeared to Solomon by night and said to him: I have heard your prayer and have chosen this place for Myself as a house of sacrifice. If I shut up heaven so no rain falls, or if I command locusts to devour the land, or if I send pestilence among My people, If My people, who are called by My name, shall humble themselves, pray, seek, crave, and require of necessity My face and turn from their wicked ways, then will I hear from heaven, forgive their sin, and heal their land. Now My eyes will be open and My ears attentive to prayer offered in this place. (2 Chron. 7:12–15) (AMP)

In each region, God has a plan. His plan is to prosper us and not harm us. His plan is revival, and that all in our cities be saved and come to the knowledge of the Truth. We must pray and give Him no rest, until His plans are established in our cities.

Set up the standard on the walls of Babylon; Make the guard strong, set up the watchmen, prepare the ambushes. (Jer. 51:12)

Your watchmen shall lift up their voices, with their voices they shall sing together; for they shall see eye to eye when the Lord brings back Zion. (Isa. 52:8)

God has strategies for ambushing the enemy. As we abide with Him and stay in unity, He will show us exactly how to defeat the enemy and what strategies to set in place. Remember, this fight is not by might, nor by power, but by the Spirit of the Lord. It is the Holy Spirit within us that sets up a standard against the enemy. He knows exactly how to bring the enemy down from his position.

As we close this chapter, I would like to talk about setting up watchmen in the local church. Those who are on staff or are volunteers over a particular area are called of God not just to a natural position, but a spiritual position as well. You are each watchmen over your particular area of ministry. As all of the staff, workers, and intercessors do their part on their side of wall, there will be no area of the church that is uncovered in prayer. The size of the ministry will determine how many positions in prayer will be filled. It is important that all our "bases" be covered.

The Unseen War

Chapter 20

He saw that there was no man, And wondered that there was no intercessor; Therefore His own arm brought salvation for Him; And His own righteousness, it sustained Him. For He put on righteousness as a breastplate, And a helmet of salvation on His head; He put on the garments of vengeance for clothing, And was clad with zeal as a cloak.

(Isa. 59:16, 17)

This scripture is speaking of Jesus. He came to the earth as an intercessor for all of mankind and to bring man back into fellowship with their Creator, God. When Jesus came to the earth, He came fully equipped. He had on the same armor as found in Ephesians 6:10–17. As stated in earlier chapters, you have authority over the devil and have on this same prayer armor. Jesus is in you, and through your prayers you are, through the name of Jesus, to be in control of the devil. He is not to control you nor the one for whom you are in intercession. (Col. 1:12, 13) This authority can also be exercised when it comes to our cities, our states, our nation and the nations of the world. After the Holy Spirit would come upon the disciples, Jesus told them they would be witnesses in Jerusalem, Judea, Samaria, and unto the uttermost parts of the world. You have authority to pray for your city, your state, and your nation, and your prayers can even reach the uttermost parts of the world. This type of focus in intercession can reach into the heavens where there are demonic strongholds over these regions. Ultimately, as you exercise this type of persistent intercession, your prayers will affect the people that live there. (Rev. 2:13; Dan. 10:12–13; 1 Tim. 2:1–8) God loves and cares for these cities and nations. His eyes look over them. He loves them because people live there.

> A land for which the Lord your God cares; the eyes of the Lord your God are always on it, from the beginning of the year to the very end of the year. (Deut. 11:12)

As you think about interceding for your region, I want you to understand the heart of God. He sits upon the circle of the earth, and sees the full picture. (Isa. 40:22) There are so many people that live in these areas that are in the valley of decision. They are blinded by demonic activity. (2 Cor. 4:4; 1 John 5:19) These cities and nations need help! I call this demonic activity a stronghold. There are different types of strongholds over different areas of the world. As you travel from one city to the next, the stronghold that affects one city may not be the same one that affects the other. As you put up your "spiritual antenna", you will be able to discern what type of demon activity is prevalent over a region. Pray for the gift of discerning of spirits. (2 Cor. 12:1–11) Ask God to reveal what is prominent over that area. Oftentimes you can look into the history of an area and discover hidden truth about the history from generation to generation. Have you ever heard the term "history repeats itself"? There is a reason for the repeating of negative, destructive history. You can give that stronghold a name as you go back into the history of an area. There is a root that needs to be pulled out, just like dandelions in a garden. If you don't get to the source, it will come back over and over. The seeds from one plant can even spread more of these unsightly weeds. These roots go very deep and it is going to take effort and the right tools to go deep into the soil, grab every bit of this root and pull it out. You can just look at the negative spiritual fruit in an area. Look at the region with your natural eyes and the eyes of your spirit. Everything that is hidden will be revealed as you ask Him for discernment. He does not want anything to be hidden to us. We are His ambassadors, and we have been called and commissioned to complete a task while here on this earth. Whatsoever we bind on earth is bound in heaven. We have the authority to do just that as we stand in the gap for these cities and nations. God is waiting for His people to come to Him and pray.

> Then the Lord appeared to Solomon by night, and said to him: "I have heard your prayer, and have chosen this place for Myself as a house of sacrifice. When I shut up heaven and there is no rain, or command the locusts to devour the land, or send pestilence among My people, if My people who are called by My name will humble themselves, and pray and seek My face, and turn from their wicked ways, then I will hear from heaven, and will forgive their sin and heal their land. Now My eyes will be open and My ears attentive to prayer made in this place. For now I have chosen and sanctified this house, that My name may be there forever; and My eyes and My heart will be there perpetually. (2 Chron. 7:12–16)

God's concern and attention are upon our regions. As an intercessor, you can stand in the gap on behalf of these regions. An intercessor takes the place of another. We can stand and ask first for forgiveness on behalf of the sin that has prevailed over that area. We can go to God and ask for grace and mercy to be extended. Where sin abounds, grace will so much more abound. (Rom. 5:20) We can boldly present this region before the throne of grace and ask that God's will be done on earth, as it is in heaven, asking Him to invade these regions with His manifested presence. Ask Him to pour out the rains of revival! (Zach. 10:1; Isa. 44:3; Joel 2) Ask that His goodness be revealed in the land of the living. The goodness of God revealed to these areas will lead to an overall spirit of repentance in that area. (Rom. 2:4) Be specific in your prayers and ask God for exactly what the Holy Spirit reveals that is needed in that area. (Isa. 62:6, 7)

After you've done all He has directed you to do in the positive side of intercession, now go after the stronghold. Go after that demonic spirit. If you want to effect change in the natural realm, go to the source. Go to the spirit realm. Go after the cause. Go after the stronghold. "The righteous take it by force."

> Finally brethren, be strong in the Lord and in the power of his might. Put on the whole armor of God, that you may be able to stand against the wiles of the devil. For we wrestle not against flesh and blood, but against principalities, against powers, against the rulers of the darkness of this age, against spiritual hosts of wickedness in high places. (Eph. 6:10–12)

You are in Jesus, and have on the breastplate of righteousness. You go in His name and cast out the devil in that region. Pull out what has been sown generation after generation. Call it out. Use the name of Jesus. "In My name you will cast out devils." Legally the land is yours; vitally it is not. You go into that area and take possession. Satan is the god of this world and he has been god over that region a long time. Don't expect him to give up his "post" easily. Be strong in the Lord, and in the power of His might. Be strong and of good courage. You are in a fight with the unseen hosts of darkness. They are principalities, powers, rulers of the darkness of this world and spiritual wickedness in high places. The Word of God teaches us that there are three heavens. There is the atmospheric heaven; it is right above us. After that there is space, where there are the stars. Then there is the third heaven where the throne of God is. (2 Cor. 12:2) Our fight is with the wicked spirits in the heavenlies, in the atmospheric realm.

You are in a battle with these unseen forces over those regions. They are wicked spirits in the heavenlies. Yes, the battle is the Lord's, but he uses you to accomplish His purposes here on this earth. You are the one who represents Jesus. We are ambassadors for Christ in this land. We go in and we take back, by our God–given spiritual force, what the enemy has taken through the fall of mankind.

> Every place that the sole of your foot will tread upon I have given you...Have I not commanded you? Be strong and of good courage; do not be afraid, nor be dismayed, for the Lord your God is with you wherever you go. (Josh. 1: 3, 9)

There is a new breed of intercessors that God has raised up in this hour. They are intercessors who know who they are in Christ and what His Word and His will are for all of mankind. They are as bold as a lion. They abide in the secret place of prayer. They abide right under the shadow of the Almighty One. They are not afraid of the terror by night; nor for the arrow that flieth by day, nor for the pestilence that walketh in darkness, nor for the destruction that wasteth at noonday. A thousand shall fall at their side and ten thousand at their right hand; but it does not come near them. (Ps. 91) They have the sword of the spirit, which is the Word of God, and they have discernment. The devil is afraid of being recognized and uncovered. These intercessors are sharpshooters. They have the precision of a well-trained soldier. They are in submission to their great leader, Jesus Christ, and they know His voice.

Intercession will slow demonic activity down. Ultimately, it will release that area from the demonic darkness so that the light of God's Word can be revealed. It also releases angelic activity over that area, thus bringing divine protection. (Heb. 1:14; Ps. 103:20; Prov. 11:11) Now remember this: these strongholds are stubborn. They have been there a long time and do not want to give up their place. You must be more stubborn than your enemy. Greater is He that is in you than he that is in the world.

Let's say I came into your house. You have a beautiful home and have worked very hard to decorate it. You have purchased furniture and have arranged it just the way you like it, the way you think looks best. Imagine if I came into your home and said, "Ok, it's all mine now. I'm taking over." I would imagine you would put up a good fight, right? You would not give up your home very easily, now would you? The devil is no different. He has been abiding over these regions a long time and he does not want to give up his house. (Matt. 12:28–29; Jude 1:20–23) These regions have been given to him at the fall of Adam. (Luke 4:5, 6) He does not want to give it up! He has worked a long time to make that region just as oppressed as he possibly can. He sees the Jesus in you coming after him. He is going to put up a fight. Your part is to be persistent; don't give up. Daniel was a man who was persistent in prayer. He did not give up until his answer came. He had been praying and was unaware that some "thing" was keeping the answer from coming. Let's read and find out what happened.

In those days I, Daniel, was mourning three full weeks. I ate no pleasant food, no meat or wine came into my mouth, nor did I anoint myself at all, till three whole weeks were fulfilled. Now on the twenty–fourth day of the first month, as I was by the side of the great river, that is, the Tigris, I lifted my eyes and looked, and behold, a certain man clothed in linen, whose waist was girded with gold of Uphaz! His body was like beryl, his face like the appearance of lightning, his eyes like torches of fire, his arms and feet like burnished bronze in color, and the sound of his words like the voice of a multitude. And I, Daniel, alone saw the vision, for the men who were with me did not see the vision; but a great terror fell upon them, so that they fled to hide themselves. Therefore I was left alone when I saw this great vision, and no strength remained in me; for my vigor was turned to frailty in me, and I retained no strength. Yet I heard the sound of his words; and while I heard the sound of his words I was in a deep sleep on my face, with my face to the ground. Suddenly, a hand touched me, which made me tremble on my knees and on the palms of my hands. And he said to me, "O Daniel, man greatly beloved, understand the words that I speak to you, and stand upright, for I have now been sent to you." While he was speaking this word to me, I stood trembling. Then he said to me, "Do not fear, Daniel, for from the first day that you set your heart to understand, and to humble yourself before your God, your words were heard; and I have come because of your words. But the prince of the kingdom of Persia withstood me twenty–one days; and behold, Michael, one of the chief princes, came to help me, for I had been left alone there with the kings of Persia. (Dan. 10:2–13)

Daniel was on a partial fast, praying and seeking God. Notice there was a time element involved in having his prayer manifest. It was three full weeks. Now the scripture tells us that the first day he began to pray, his prayer was heard but there was a hindrance in the heavenlies trying to keep his prayer from manifesting. "The prince of the kingdom of Persia withstood me." This prince was a spirit being. He was trying to keep the message from Daniel, so God had to send reinforcements, Michael the archangel, to help get the angel through to Daniel. King Cyrus was the natural king in that time. He was a man who was the king of Persia. The prince of Persia was a spirit being. He was in the heavenlies. King Cyrus was the natural ruler, and then there was a satanic ruler in the unseen realm. Our fight is not with flesh and blood; our fight is with these rulers in the heavenlies.

> For I want you to know what a great conflict I have for you and those in Laodicea, and for as many as have not seen my face in the flesh... For though I am absent in the flesh, yet I am with you in spirit, rejoicing to see your good order and the steadfastness of your faith in Christ. (Col. 2:1, 5)

The word "conflict" in the Greek is the word *agon*. It means a race against spiritual foes, as well as human adversaries. He was doing this in the spirit. In prayer, he was absent from them in the flesh, but present with them in the spirit.

God's plans for these cities and nations are to prosper them and give them a hope and a future in His presence. (Jer. 29:11) After we have stood in repentance on behalf of these regions, and reminded God of His desire toward these regions, we can pray in tongues. The areas we don't know, the Holy Spirit knows. He knows just how to pray to help us gain the victory over these demons. We don't fight spiritual battles with natural, carnal weapons. We fight them with the weapons of our warfare. Discernment, the Word of God and tongues are the weapons God has given us to over come the enemy. Tongues go into the unseen realm, grab hold of that spirit and wrestle it to the ground. An experienced intercessor will know when this is happening. There are some things about intercession that are better "caught than taught". As you are praying, the tongues are forceful. I've been in intercession where after going to the throne of God and speaking and believing His word on behalf of a region, began to pray in the spirit. As I was praying in tongues, I was praying out the mind, will and government of God for that region, when my tongues would switch into more forceful tongues, where I was wrestling in prayer. I am not wrestling with God, for He would that all men be saved and come to the knowledge of the truth. He desires that His character be revealed to these cities. But I was coming up against demonic strongholds. I am very aware when this is happening. It's different; it feels different and sounds different. I'm "caught up" more with the spiritual realm than I am the natural realm, and very aware of spiritual things. I find myself in and out of tongues, and using the name of Jesus and commanding the devil to release the object of my prayer. This can happen not just in intercession for a region, but also on behalf of a person. You know when you've come up against a demonic force as you're praying. There is a wrestling going on. You also can, at times, sense the weight of the darkness. That is not the time to quit praying. Pray until you get the release. If you don't have time and have to leave your place of prayer, make sure your end your time of intercession with worship so that you are filled back up and refreshed.

> See, I have this day set you over the nations and over the kingdoms, To root out and to pull down, To destroy and to throw down, To build and to plant. (Jer. 1:10)

As watchmen, we stand on the walls of our cities and nations. We have authority to destroy the works of the devil and pull down these strongholds that are in the heavenlies. Then the ground is prepared, and through the teaching of the Word of God, these areas can be built up. Does this sound too good to be true? Does this sound like a dream?

> Look among the nations and watch— Be utterly astounded! For I will work a work in your days which you would not believe, though it were told you. (Hab. 1:5)

Identification in Intercession

Chapter 21

Rejoice with those who rejoice (sharing others' joy) and weep with those who weep (sharing others' grief).
(Rom. 12:15) (AMP)

An intercessor is one who takes the place of another. There are times in intercession where the love of God grips your spirit and you enter into deep identification with another person's infirmities. No, you don't take it on in the flesh, or in your human body. No, you don't become sick for them; Jesus already bore the sicknesses. No, you don't become depressed and walk around with another person's depression. Inwardly, while caught in the grips of deep intercession, you identify with that person and in your spirit you can "feel" their pain. While in this place of prayer, the deepest part of you is calling and meeting with the deepest part of God and you are so gripped with their pain, you will not let go of God's mercy until relief comes. You will know when it comes. Remember what I said earlier? Some things are better "caught than taught". The Holy Spirit, by your human spirit, picks up on that person's need, and so grips your inner man that you are touched deeply by the feelings of their infirmity. No, you are not Jesus, but Jesus the intercessor is alive within you, and loves that person unconditionally and wants them to be set free and delivered. This deep identification does not always happen every time you are in intercession. The Holy Spirit has, at this point, anointed you to pray this thing through to victory. Oftentimes, the word of wisdom or the word of knowledge is in operation at this point. Because of this anointing, and your sensitivity to the Spirit, you will be able to have understanding of the person's grief, infirmity, pain or suffering.

Let me give you an example. A friend of mine went through a very hard time in his life. I decided by an act of my will to take on this prayer assignment. This particular prayer assignment was born out of my desire to help this individual and his family. I took his need to the word of God. I prayed out the scriptures that met his need. I then began to pray in tongues for him because I didn't know what exactly God's will was for his situation. "He who searches the hearts of men knows what is in the mind of the (Holy) Spirit (what His intent is), because the Spirit intercedes and pleads (before God) in behalf of the saints according to and in harmony with God's will." (Rom. 8:27) (AMP) The Holy Spirit is there with us to aid and assist us in our prayers. He knows the needs, and He knows how to get the job done. You are the vessel of honor that He is flowing through at the moment. As I prayed for him in tongues, I noticed the manifested presence of the Holy Spirit. He was supernaturally getting involved. You can be more anointed or less anointed to pray. Whether you feel anything or not, your prayers avail much. (James 5:16) At this moment, I sensed the Holy Spirit's anointing flowing though me as I prayed. As I yielded to Him, I found myself saying, "I'm so sad." Internally, I felt the sorrow and the grief of this individual for whom I was praying. I personally was not sad or depressed, but I continued again in tongues. As I continued, I felt the weight of this person's sadness. This revelation came by the Holy Spirit through the word of knowledge, but even more came as I continued praying. I knew instantly that I was not praying for my friend, but for his youngest son. I had natural knowledge that he had children, but no natural knowledge of how many or their gender. What I knew now by revelation was that his youngest son was in deep sadness, to the point of depression. I also knew at that moment the nature of this child's relationship with his father. Both he and the child were emotionally connected and there was a need for communication. All this revelation came in an instant. I continued to pray over a period of several days for my friend. The Bible says to "prove all things", so I emailed my friend and asked him if he had any children and how old and how many. He told me. When I read the e-mail, I learned the name of his youngest son. Because of my relationship with this friend, and the mutual respect we share, I very gently began to share with him what the Lord had showed me. Because my friend was already in a lot of emotional pain himself, I was very gentle and wise as to how much I shared with him. I did not want to cause him any more pain. Fortunately, he was open and I took his youngest child on as another prayer assignment. After a period of time, communication between this father and his son was restored. Some of the pain and sadness has also been relieved. Love never fails a prayer assignment. His love must motivate you to continue steadfast, unmovable in this work of intercession until God releases you to the next assignment. This type of identification in intercession helped to bring about deliverance and restoration. God is the Author and Finisher of their faith and He will bring to completion all things in their life as He wills. Our job is to obey the Master and follow his directions.

Paul identified with the Jews that he might gain the Jews. To the weak, he became weak that he might gain the weak. He said that he was made all things to all men that he by all means saves some. (1 Cor. 9:19–22)

Through identification in intercession, you are bringing about deliverance. Remember Romans 15:1? We, then, that are strong, ought to bear the infirmities of the weak. That word "bear" means to lift up with the idea of completely removing it from another person.

The members should have the same care for another. And whether one member suffers, all the members suffer with it; or the one member be honored, all the members rejoice with it. (1 Cor. 12:25, 26)

> All of us as members, one of another, ought to have the same care for each other. Prayer is the support for one another in our time of need. We all are not strong at the same time.

Interceding with the Help
of the Holy Spirit

Chapter 22

So too the (Holy) Spirit comes to our aid and bears us up in our weakness; for we do not know what prayer to offer nor how to offer it worthily as we ought, but the Spirit Himself goes to meet our supplication and pleads in our behalf with unspeakable yearnings and groanings too deep for utterance. And He who searches the hearts of men knows what is in the mind of the (Holy) Spirit (what His intent is), because the Spirit intercedes and pleads (before God) in behalf of the saints according to and in harmony with God's will. (Rom. 8:26–27)

We have seen that intercession can be prayed with the understanding and in the spirit, also known as "praying in tongues". I call this level of intercession the first level. This level of intercession is effective and produces results as we have already seen. There are times, however, when intercession goes to another level and you enter into what I call a second level. This type of prayer is not worked up emotionally; it is initiated by the person of the Holy Spirit. There is a deep inner working and words (whether in praying the Scriptures or praying in tongues) are not sufficient in getting the spiritual release needed to accomplish the purposes of God. As you enter into this second level, your intercessions become unspeakable yearnings too deep for words. It means praying with "with sighs too deep for words". (RSV) In this place of prayer, you feel as if your heart is going to break. The deepest part of you is calling and meeting with the deepest part of God. There is inner groaning and tears.

In this level of intercession there is compassion, and you feel as if you are giving birth. Like a woman in labor, she not only groans because of her labor pains, but also with desire to bring forth the child! This is not just pain; it is the pain that is transfigured by longing, by hope and expectation. There is identification. There is suffering, but its nature is spiritual, bringing with it some physical accompaniments. At this level of intercession, your prayers are uttered in inarticulate sounds. This level of prayer is as private as a woman giving birth to a baby. You do not feel comfortable praying this way in public. It is for the private moments with God or with church "family" who understand the inner workings of the Spirit of God. He will not be mocked. He is very sensitive, and flows through those intercessors who are open to "all" of who He is and what He is capable of accomplishing through His ministry.

Many shut their mind off to what sounds irrational or incomprehensible. It is not irrational; like so many other things in the realm of the spirit, it is super–rational. What is natural to God is unnatural to man. Faith is not rational, believing something that is not as though it is. (Heb. 11:1; Rom. 10:17) This is the language of the Spirit. (John 15:19) The things of the Spirit do not always look the way the natural man would expect; just take a moment and read through the book of Revelation! You are not of this world! Many have grieved the Holy Spirit and mocked him in regards to this kind of praying. This level of prayer is called the "art of intercession" and if we are not careful, we will lose this level of intercession in the modem day church. That is why we must teach on it, but with the understanding that the Holy Spirit is the enabler. He is the one who knows the times and seasons that God has planned for all things. (Eccles. 3) To everything there is a season, and a time to every purpose under heaven. There is a time to speak the word, and a time to pray in tongues. There is a time to stand in repentance. There is a time to go with the breastplate of righteousness and boldly decree and declare the finished work of God for a person or a region. There is also a time to be born. There will be no births without true groanings and travail. That which is born of the flesh is flesh; that which is born of the Spirit is spirit.

Be sensitive to the Holy Spirit and His leading as you intercede. The more you enter into the secret chamber with him, the more you will experience the different levels of intercession. Don't be afraid of it and don't cast your pearls before someone who will not understand the way He is working through you in intercession. He is the one leading you.

> The sheep hear his voice; and he calls his own sheep by name and leads them out. (John 10:3)

> However, when He, the Spirit of truth, has come, He will guide you into all truth; for He will not speak on His own authority, but whatever He hears He will speak; and He will tell you things to come. 14 He will glorify Me, for He will take of what is Mine and declare it to you. (John 16:13, 14)

> For as many as are led by the Spirit of God, these are sons of God. (Rom. 8:14)

> But the anointing which you have received from Him abides in you, and you do not need that anyone teach you; but as the same anointing teaches you concerning all things, and is true, and is not a lie, and just as it has taught you, you will abide in Him. (1 John 2:27)

There was a season in the early eighties when God had called me to go across the nation and teach His people how to pray. We know there are all manner of prayer, but He specifically told me to teach the church the art of intercession. We raised up many intercessors and helped many churches pioneer their prayer groups. After teaching the Word of God on the first level of intercession and what it would accomplish, at times, if the church I was speaking at was ready, I taught on groanings and travail. The anointing was there to teach it, but there came a time when the Holy Spirit was grieved and He told me and others to stop ministering this word. He was grieved, so the anointing on this message lifted.

As time went on, I found out that there was much "talk" and doubt on this particular subject. Even Jesus Himself could do no mighty works in his own country because of unbelief. (Matt. 13:58) The Holy Spirit will not go where He is not welcome. If the church wants to reject His ministry and labor in the flesh, He will not stop us. He will let us go until we cry out to Him with clean hands and a pure heart and finally realize that our thoughts are not His thoughts and His ways are not our ways. We must follow His formula for success because He is the one that understands the spirit realm and how it operates. Yes, a few intercessors got off and went on in the flesh, but the price we paid was that we lost the genuine. Because we are living in a dry and thirsty land, we again desire Him to help us in our prayers.

Spiritual Birth through Travail

Chapter 23

Ask of Me, and I will give You The nations for Your inheritance. (Ps. 2:8)

God's will and desire is that all men be saved and come to the knowledge of the Truth. His will is that not one perishes. (1 Tim 2:4) His desire is that many sons and daughters come into the realm of eternity with Him in heaven. He is the Father of Love and He is not satisfied; He wants more children. As intercessors, we will not deny Him of His heart's desire. We will line our desire up with His desire and pray His will be done. His desire is sons and daughters, not conversions. The Bible says "you must be born-again". (John 3:5–8) He wants birth. You cannot have birth without having travail. A baby does not give birth to itself! An intercessor is the one who gives birth.

> Before she was in labor, she gave birth; Before her pain came, She delivered a male child. Who has heard such a thing? Who has seen such things? Shall the earth be made to give birth in one day? Or shall a nation be born at once? For as soon as Zion was in labor, She gave birth to her children. Shall I bring to the time of birth, and not cause delivery? says the Lord. Shall I who cause delivery shut up the womb? says your God. (Isa. 66:7–9)

We know this scripture is speaking of Israel, but there is also a spiritual application. Israel will be reborn as a nation in the natural, and in the spiritual, Zion will be the one who will travail and bring forth her children. Zion is the church. (Heb. 12:18–23) The scripture says, "as soon as Zion travailed, she brought forth her children".

As you enter into travail and groaning, you yourself will identify with the lost. You will feel lost and hopeless, even though you are saved. There will be at times intense weeping. Worship feels good, but this type of intercession has sorrow, sadness toil and labor. Pray until you get the release. There will be joy and singing. Just like when a woman gives birth to a baby, there is labor, sadness and groaning, but at the birth, there is joy!

> My little children, of whom I travail in birth again until
> Christ be formed in you. (Gal. 4:19) (KJV)

Paul travailed first for them to be saved and then again for Christ to be formed in them. It is one thing for Christ to be in us, and another thing for Christ to be formed in us. There is a comparison between natural growth and spiritual growth. When a person is born again, he is a babe. (1 Pet. 2:2) He needs to mature. Paul was interceding for the churches of Galicia because they were trying to get back under the law. God wanted them to walk in freedom and fulfill His plan for their lives.

> Epaphras, who is one of you, a bondservant of Christ,
> greets you, always laboring fervently for you in prayers,
> that you may stand perfect and complete in all the will
> of God. For I bear him witness that he has a great zeal
> for you, and those who are in Laodicea, and those in
> Hierapolis. (Col. 4:12–13)

The word "laboring" is the Greek word *panos*. The meaning denotes labor, toil, and the consequence of toil, distress, suffering and pain. The word "zeal" is also the same word, *panos*. (*W.E. Vine's Expository Dictionary of New Testament Words*) He was laboring for them in prayer that they would stand perfect and complete in all the will of God! God's will was that they move forward in their destiny.

Tears in Intercession

Chapter 24

Oh, that my head were waters, And my eyes a fountain of tears, that I might weep day and night for the slain daughter of my people! (Jer. 9:1)

*J*eremiah was known as the weeping prophet. He saw the backslidden condition of the people. What he saw affected his heart! He was weeping for the sins of the people! He was weeping for their backslidden state. They were out of God's will and coming under the bondage of the enemy. As you read the book of Jeremiah, you will discover that there was hardness in their hearts. This rebellion against God's ways and authority produced not only physical death, but spiritual death as well. To change their condition, there was a call for weeping and mourning.

> Thus says the Lord of hosts: "Consider and call for the mourning women, That they may come; And send for skillful wailing women, That they may come. Let them make haste And take up a wailing for us, That our eyes may run with tears, And our eyelids gush with water. For a voice of wailing is heard from Zion: 'How we are plundered! We are greatly ashamed, Because we have forsaken the land, Because we have been cast out of our dwellings.'" Yet hear the word of the Lord, O women, And let your ear receive the word of His mouth; Teach your daughters wailing, And everyone

her neighbor a lamentation. For death has come through our windows, Has entered our palaces, To kill off the children— no longer to be outside! And the young men— no longer on the streets! (Jer. 9:17–21)

There is the same cry in the spirit today, a call for humility and prayer so that God can heal our land; the weeping of repentance from the heart on behalf of the spiritually dead in our land. Those who wait for the Light, but behold obscurity; for brightness, but they walk in darkness. Those who grope for the wall like the blind, and grope as if they had no eyes; they stumble at noonday as in the night, those who are in desolate places as dead men. Those who don't know the way of peace, they speak oppression and revolt, conceiving and uttering falsehood from their hearts. He saw that there was no man, and wondered where the intercessors were. (Isa. 59) Oh, that our heads were waters and our eyes a fountain of tears! God, give us tears for the lost! May we see as You see! God, Your eyes run to and from the whole earth, to show Yourself true to those who sit in darkness! Lord, call forth the mourning men and women! Call forth the intercessors! Anoint them with fresh oil! Do it, God, for your sake and for the sake of all those who are yet to be saved. May those who are marked for intercession run into the secret place and pray, and not grow weary and faint. May they stand and pray without ceasing, until Your will is accomplished here on this earth, as it is in heaven. May Your intercessors run with the vision!

Weeping is for both men and women. In the world, weeping is a sign of weakness. Weeping, in the Holy Spirit, is precious and powerful. It is an expression of His heart, His emotions and nature. This weeping in prayer also softens the heart of the intercessor. These moments, connected with eternity, are like treasures to be stored up in our book of memories as intimate times with God.

I want you to notice that the scripture in Jeremiah 9 said to call forth "skillful" women. It is important for the intercessor to be skillful in handling his or her emotions. You don't have to be burdened down with the needs of others. It is important that you do not take anything on in your soul. Keep your intercessions in the Spirit, and as you go about your daily affairs, be joyful! He said, "I'll make them joyful in My house of prayer!" God also laughs and wants us to enjoy life to its fullness. (Ps. 2:4; John 10:10)

The Birth of a Miracle

Chapter 25

Therefore, when Jesus saw her weeping, and the Jews who came with her weeping, He groaned in the spirit and was troubled. And He said, "Where have you laid him?" They said to Him, "Lord, come and see." Jesus wept. Then the Jews said, "See how He loved him!" And some of them said, "Could not this Man, who opened the eyes of the blind, also have kept this man from dying?" Then Jesus, again groaning in Himself, came to the tomb. It was a cave, and a stone lay against it. Jesus said, "Take away the stone." Martha, the sister of him who was dead, said to Him, "Lord, by this time there is a stench, for he has been dead four days." Then they took away the stone from the place where the dead man was lying. And Jesus lifted up His eyes and said, "Father, I thank You that You have heard Me. And I know that You always hear Me, but because of the people who are standing by I said this, that they may believe that You sent Me." Now when He had said these things, He cried with a loud voice, "Lazarus, come forth!" And he who had died came out bound hand and foot with graveclothes, and his face was wrapped with a cloth. Jesus said to them, "Loose him, and let him go." (John 11:33–39, 41–44)

When Jesus arrived, the atmosphere was charged with confusion, doubt, unbelief and religion. In walks, the King of kings and the Lord of lords. He is the Resurrection and the Life. (John 11:25) Jesus is also filled with the Holy Spirit. (Luke 4:1) The Holy Spirit is active in His life and ministry. He knows the voice of His Father. He understands the spirit realm. Lazarus had been dead four days. You can't get any deader than that! The situation looks completely impossible from the natural, earthly standpoint. "With man it is impossible, but with God all things are possible". (Matt. 19:26) And all things are possible to believing, prevailing prayers! The effects of death had settled in to such a degree that Martha, Lazarus's sister, said, "Lord by this time he stinketh!" Yes, death stinks. Sin stinks. Spiritual death stinks! But there is hope for the lost! There is hope for the bound! Faith is the substance of things hoped for! We can't give up on anyone. Not ever! Hope deferred makes the heart sick. (Prov. 13:12) Many intercessors give up right before the birth of their miracle, right when the vision is about to be born. Usually that is when the circumstances become more challenging.

Discouragement is an enemy to our prayers. Don't allow your mind to become distracted with this enemy! You've been praying and believing for a long time. "Remember, there is a time to be born! ...though the vision tarries, wait for it!" (Hab. 2:3)

Many intercessors give up right at the point of birth. They abort the very thing that was assigned to them to carry out to completion. Remember what God said. "Shall I bring to the birth, and shut up the womb?" He will bring to pass the birth of this miracle. Spiritual pride says God can't complete what He has started. We must fall on our face and repent for our own doubt and unbelief. We, too, must take heed, lest we fall into these traps. (1 Cor. 10:12) God is both the Author and the Finisher of what He has begun. Time is also an enemy of intercessors. Martha said, "He's been dead four days." So what? Eternity knows no time or distance. The spirit realm is not made up of a time element. Don't look at how long this process has been going on; look unto Jesus.

Jesus was filled with the Holy Spirit, and every gift was in operation in His life and ministry except tongues and interpretation of tongues. (1 Cor. 12:7–11, 14:1–28; Mark 16:17; Jude 1:20) The manifestation of tongues is for this dispensation only; after the birth of the church age, tongues became a manifestation of the infilling of the Holy Spirit.

Now Jesus, filled with the Holy Spirit, looks at the situation before Him. He chooses to yield to the Holy Spirit and flow in whatever expression was needed to bring about the deliverance of this person who was held captive in the grips of death. "He groaned in the spirit, and was troubled." He groaned in the spirit, He yielded to the Spirit of grace and supplication. At this moment, groaning is exactly the expression that was needed to bring forth deliverance. The time had come to deliver Lazarus from death. Then Jesus asked, "Where have you laid him?" Then He wept. Was He weeping in identification for the ones that had lost a family member, or was He weeping in the spirit because of their unbelief? They thought he was weeping because of soulish reasons. "Behold, how He loved him." But Jesus walked in the Spirit, not yielding to the dictates of the flesh. He was weeping in the Spirit! Jesus then walked toward the tomb where Lazarus was laid. As He was approaching, He again groaned, sighed from deep within. He was about to raise the dead. He tells them to roll away the stone. He is about to bring the glory of God into this seemingly impossible situation. His prayers have availed much, even though there have been no words, just groaning, sighs and weeping. Jesus then lifts up His eyes, and says, "Father, I thank thee that you have heard me, and I know that you hear me always". He knew His prayer had pushed out the darkness and death. He cries with a loud voice, "Lazarus, come forth!" A miracle comes forth. Lazarus is raised from the dead!

> Even when we were dead in trespasses, made us alive together with Christ (by grace you have been saved), and raised us up together, and made us sit together in the heavenly places in Christ Jesus. (Eph. 2:5, 6)

He is raised from the dead, but there is still one more area of relief for Lazarus. Jesus sees that he is wrapped in grave clothes. He can't loose himself. He needs someone to do it for him. He can't move around freely and enjoy his new life. He is still bound up. Jesus commands them to loose him and let him go.

Jesus was a man of unshakable faith, knowing there is no time or distance in the Spirit. He chose to wait two more days in the place where He was. Though Jesus knew by revelation that Lazarus was dead, that did not move Him. He was confident in the fact that what God begins, He will complete. He was confident that He had the power to raise Lazarus from the dead. You, as an intercessor, must have the same unshakable faith. Your prayers will produce life where there is death. Yielding to the Holy Spirit in groaning will produce life, thus giving birth to a miracle.

Is There a Watchman in the House?

Chapter 26

Behold, children are a heritage from the Lord, the fruit of the womb is a reward. Like arrows in the hand of a warrior, So are the children of one's youth. (Ps. 127:3–4)

I had been having trouble conceiving, so my husband and I decided seek professional help from a doctor who specialized in invitro fertilization. During the nine-day invitro cycle, I was feeling upset that this was the road I had to take in order to have the desire of my heart, which was to have children. I was asking God, "What is going on?" Just as I was pulling my car into my garage, God spoke to me and said, "You are going to have twins in your first pregnancy and a singleton in your second. In your first pregnancy you will conceive through invitro fertilization. In your second pregnancy you will get pregnant on your own". I wrote it down and to this day still have the original piece of paper. Needless to say, I became pregnant on the first invitro cycle that we attempted. At about twenty-five weeks, I was put on complete bed rest and given special medication that would help to stop or hinder early dilation and contractions. Thirty weeks and three day in utero, I went into pre-term labor. After being hospitalized for several hours, the doctors thought it was in the best interest of the children to perform a C-section, for they would not have survived a "natural" childbirth. Ready or not, these babies were coming.

We knew the circumstances of their birth were not ideal, for they were going to arrive almost ten weeks early. When the doctors went in to get Jonathan, he came out screaming. He was breathing fine, and his weight was three pounds, five ounces. When they went in to get Danielle, she came out quietly, and was only three pounds. At first she was not breathing. During the whole delivery my family was praying for them. We were standing on the promises of God. I kept reminding God of His *rhema* word to me. "Father, you said in my first pregnancy I would give birth to two babies. I thank You for Your promises, that not only would I be the happy mother of twins, but that they would be healthy." (Ps. 113:9) I also reminded Him of His promises concerning healing on their behalf. This was the beginning of my calling to be not just their natural mother, give birth and to them raise them, but I would be their spiritual mother as well, whereby I would shape them for God and aid and assist in giving birth to their destinies. My home church found out about their premature birth, and they too agreed with us in prayer. The day they were born, all my closest friends had come to what was supposed to be my baby shower! They too were praying for their health. Everyone we knew and people we didn't know prayed the prayer of agreement and intercession on their behalf.

During their six-week stay in the hospital, The Holy Spirit revealed to me several things about their future. He gave me several scriptures for each of them. I put the scriptures on plaques for their bedrooms. These are scriptures as it relates to their individual destinies, but not specific ones. The specifics regarding their destinies are hidden in my heart, for I will never tell them. The specifics are up to them to discover for themselves.

Seven months after the birth of my twins, I found out I was a full twenty weeks pregnant. What a surprise! Nineteen weeks later, I gave birth to another daughter whom we named Jaclyn. God began to speak to me when she was about six months old. Again, He gave me several scriptures as it relates to her future and a sense about a particular talent (bent) He wanted me to encourage. (Prov. 22:6) I wrote the scriptures for her on a plaque and put them in her room as well. More specific revelations about Jaclyn did not come to me until she was about nine years old and again these things are hidden in my heart.

I don't know why God chooses to work one way with one child and another way with another. It is up to Him to know the times and seasons of revelation. As parents, He shows us things to come so that we can pray and prepare the way for them in the Spirit. He does not show us things about our children for us to tell them. Their own purposes must be found out on their own, and in God's time and their time. Let the kids be kids. Teach them the Word, involve them in a local church and stay in the secret place of prayer on their behalf, praying that their faith fail not; praying that they would have the wisdom to choose the proper friends; praying for their future, that God would form the right mate for them. Remember, your prayers are eternal, and long after you've left this earth, they will continue to avail much in their lives.

> She rejoices over the future (the later day or time to come, knowing that she and her family are in readiness for it)! ... She looks well to how things go in her household. (Prov. 31:25, 27)

These scriptures are speaking about a virtuous woman. A praying woman is a virtuous woman. She fears the Lord and trusts in His promises. While this scripture speaks specifically to a woman's natural and spiritual role in the home, a man can also be included as I relate it to intercession for your family. The scripture tells us that she rejoices over the future because preparation has been made for her family's future. We prepare our children for their future through education in the natural and education in the Word of God. We can also prepare them for their future by supporting by them in prayer. We found out that intercession prepares the way, makes "ready" a highway for our God. "Father God, go before the path of my children, and prepare the way before them. Give them friends after Your own heart." I have prayed that prayer countless times for my children, especially when we were in the middle of a move in location. As a mother, my desire was for it to go as smoothly for them as possible. I would pack, organize, make arrangements for the utilities, and I would pray. We are not alone or without help as we journey through this world. We have not because we ask not. So I would ask in English, and then I would pray for them in tongues.

When all three children were in preschool, we had one such move in location. Every night for about five months, I prayed that God would go before us and prepare the way. We had been living in our new location for about one and a half years when it was time for kindergarten orientation for Jaclyn. She met her teacher and got to ride on a big bus.

Jaclyn sat next to a little girl named Anna. They talked to each other and enjoyed each other's company. When Jaclyn got in my car, she told me how she had made a new friend named Anna. She was very excited and a little less nervous knowing that she had made a new friend. A week later, school was officially in session and Anna and Jaclyn were assigned to sit across from each other at the table. They also found out that they shared a cubby! Several weeks later I was introduced to Anna's mother. She said she knew me from my home church, and that I was speaking at a service where she was in attendance. At the time, she had no children and was having trouble conceiving. She told me she had come up for prayer and I prayed for her. Shortly after that service she conceived her first child and named her Bessy. A few years later she conceived again, and little Anna was born! Now here we are! I moved to a completely different town, our paths crossed, and our daughters meet at school! Intercession prepares the way and makes the crooked ways straight and the rough places plain! This type of prayer aids in lining things up! This little girl continues to be my daughter's best friend, and Anna is a precious Christian girl. We have since moved again, and Anna and Jaclyn continue to remain very close (best of) friends. I know they will be there for each other as they experience peer pressure, and all the other things that are involved in growing up. Anna's mother has become one of my closest friends as well. God's Word works, and so do the effectual prayers of a righteous parent.

In the days we live, there is a lot of pressure on our children. As parents, we could get concerned for them if we did not remember that they were born to live in such a time as this. Those whom God calls, He equips. These children are equipped to handle these, as some call it, "last days." Who would have ever thought that many mothers here in New York and New Jersey, including myself, would have to go and pick up their children on September 11, 2001 from school because we didn't know what was going to happen next? We live in a different world today, and our children need our prayer support. Just like us, they are in a race. (Heb. 12:1–2) I choose to be a supportive parent, both in the natural and in the spirit. I desire that they successfully run the race that is set before them. We often hear from the teachers at the public school that parental support is necessary to ensure that your children have a positive learning experience. The same holds true with their walk with God and fulfillment of their God-given destiny. Their destiny is not measured by their career choices. I am talking about our children being free from the effects of this world's system. Free from drugs. Free from premarital sex, and the deadly diseases that follow wrong choices.

While we are conscious about getting our children to their sports practice or next dance class, let's be conscious that we can effect change in their lives with what is done in the secret place. You don't even have to tell them you're praying for them. Oftentimes, I take the specific scriptures that God has given to me for each of my children, and I bring them before God in prayer. One child at a time, I pray those *rhema* scriptures, and then pray for each of them in tongues. We may know some things regarding our children's future, but we only know "words" about what is in store for them. Again, that is where praying in tongues comes in. God is the Alpha and the Omega. He knows your children's futures from beginning to end. Nothing that happens will take Him by surprise. Before they were formed in the womb, God knew them and ordained a plan for their lives. To us, their lives are like a mystery book. Have you ever read a good mystery book? You may have been given a few clues along the way, but those clues were not the whole picture! Just when you thought you had it all figured out, here comes another clue! You have to walk by faith, knowing that God is perfecting everything that concerns your children. While I may have a few specific clues for each of my children, their futures to me are still a mystery, but not to God. The Bible says that he that speaks in an unknown tongue speaks not unto men but unto God, for in the Spirit he speaks mysteries. When you pray for them in tongues, you are praying out the mystery! When we enter eternity as a family, we will see that what we have done on this earth will have its effect in eternity.

The Proverbs 31 scripture also says, "she looks well to how things go in her household." This speaks to me about discernment, having discernment in your own household! You are the watchman on the walls of your own household. You look well as to how things are going. You can see trouble coming from afar. There are times I have a sense of impeding danger. I'm troubled in my spirit, or I may even have a dream involving one of my children. Bind it up and pray! You can stop things from happening. God's desire is to keep your children protected from harm. A child may have a "bent" toward a talent or gifting. He or she can also have a bent in certain areas of sin. Pray for them. Don't pray the problem;

pray the answer. Replace that bent with scriptures that will fill that gap in their lives.

> And all your (spiritual) children shall be disciples (taught by the Lord and obedient to His will), and great shall be the peace and undisturbed composure of your children. (Isa. 54:13) (AMP)

I have a friend who has a daughter in college and almost every time I was in my friend's presence, even though she has two other children, this one daughter would come up. I had what I call "the concern of the Holy Ghost" for her. I didn't want to tell my friend, but I sensed impending danger. I would tell my friend to pray Psalms 91 over her daughter.

This went on for a couple of years! While I would pray for her daughter myself, a mother's responsibility was to pray for her own daughter. We are watchmen over our own households! Recently, my friend called me and told me someone had attempted to rape her in her dorm. Not even someone on campus, but a stranger from outside had somehow broke into the dorm! Her daughter's courage and boldness was the strength in the time of this trouble! She was even able to pick the person out by going through mug shots at the police station.

Because of my relationship with this mother, I took her daughter as one of my "kids." I have other children whom my children have a relationship with that are "mine" too. I "adopt" them. I tell them I'm your "godmother"! I have a heart for these children and pray for them as I see needs arising. You can have spiritual children as well, and they may not even be born of your womb.

> Sing, O barren, You who have not borne! Break forth into singing, and cry aloud, You who have not labored with child! For more are the children of the desolate Than the children of the married woman, says the Lord. (Isa. 54:1)

You are also watchmen over your blood family. You can believe God for the salvations of your family members. God will be faithful to warn you of impending danger for them as well.

Believe on the Lord Jesus Christ, and you will be saved,
you and your household. (Acts 16:31)

The word "saved" is the Greek word *sozo*. It means to save, i.e. deliver
or protect, heal, preserve, do well, make whole. Do you believe that? I
claim this scripture for all my relatives, all of them. They are not living
with me in my home, but they are my family, and I expect to be warned
by the Holy Spirit if there is something that needs prayer. Over the years,
these prayer alarms have gone off in my spirit. Stay sensitive to the Holy
Spirit, and expect Him to do great and mighty things in your family.

Some Final Words

I started this book by praying for you and I am going to end with a Prayer for you. I bow my knees to the Father of our Lord Jesus Christ, from whom the whole family in heaven and earth is named, that He would grant you, according to the riches of His glory, to be strengthened with might through His Spirit in the inner man, that Christ may dwell in your heart through faith; that you, being rooted and grounded in love, may be able to comprehend with all the saints what *is* the width and length and depth and height— to know the love of Christ which passes knowledge; that you may be filled with all the fullness of God. Now to Him who is able to do exceedingly abundantly above all that you ask or think, according to the power that works in you, to Him *be* glory in the church by Christ Jesus to all generations, forever and ever. Amen.

CPSIA information can be obtained at www.ICGtesting.com
Printed in the USA
BVOW08s0953210814

363693BV00006B/114/P